SPOTLIGHT

LOUISVILLE & THE BOURBON TRAIL

THERESA DOWELL BLACKINTON

Contents

LOUISVILLE & THE BOURBON TRAIL

LOUISVILLE

Louisville (pronounce it LUH-vul if you want to sound like a local) is where the Fortune 500 meet the nation's largest high school football game, where the first Saturday in May is marked by designer duds and ostentatious hats as well as cut-off shorts and bikini tops, and where the country's best Victorian-era preservation district gets along neighborly with striking modern architecture.

Even to those who call it home, Louisville is a conundrum and a contradiction. It's a big city, the biggest in Kentucky, but it's also city of neighborhoods where everyone is connected by far less than six degrees of separation. A hint of Midwestern modesty and Northern sensibility season the city's personality, thanks to its location at the falls of the Ohio River, but Southern hospitality is still the prevailing ingredient.

Built on the backs of Irish, German, and other European immigrants as well as enslaved Africans, Louisville has also been influenced by Hispanic culture, as well as the traditions of more recent immigrants and refugees from Eastern Europe and Asia. In a state that paints itself red every election season, Louisville remains a solid dot of blue.

On paper, Louisville might not make sense, but hey, neither does love, and that's exactly what residents and visitors alike feel for the city. For some, the passion stems from Louisville's big-city amenities. The Derby City is home to a performing arts scene that supports one of the nation's most respected theater festivals, so many art galleries as to require two monthly trolley hops, research hospitals that perform groundbreaking work like the first hand

© THERESA DOWELL BLACKINTON

HIGHLIGHTS

◖ **Louisville Slugger Museum & Factory:** Witness the transformation of a piece of ash wood into an iconic Louisville Slugger baseball bat on the factory tour, then relive magical moments in the history of America's pastime in the museum (page 13).

◖ **Muhammad Ali Center:** Far beyond a simple celebration of the boxing prowess of the self-proclaimed "Greatest," this multimedia museum explores Ali's controversial struggles as well as his humanitarian acts. It is a must whether you're a boxing fan or not (page 17).

◖ **Old Louisville Tours:** The nation's best preserved Victorian neighborhood, Old Louisville brims with houses that will make your jaw drop. Take a tour to really dive into the history and architecture of the area, or spend the night in one of the neighborhood's grand B&Bs (page 19).

◖ **Kentucky Derby Museum and Churchill Downs:** Churchill Downs brims with atmosphere as the most historic thoroughbred racetrack in the world, and the adjoining Kentucky Derby Museum lets you experience the thrill of the races even when the track is dark (page 21).

◖ **Louisville Zoo:** An award-winning gorilla exhibit brought the Louisville Zoo to the forefront for animal lovers, but the new arctic animals exhibit and the much loved Islands exhibit mean the gorillas have to share the spotlight (page 27).

◖ **First Friday Trolley Hop:** Downtown's Main and Market Streets are home to an ever-expanding population of art galleries, all of which can be explored via trolley on the first Friday of the month, when many galleries host openings, offer snacks and drinks, and make artists available for conversation (page 33).

◖ **Kentucky Derby Festival:** The most exciting two minutes in sports (also known as the Kentucky Derby) cap off not only a day of glamour, madness, and myth at Churchill Downs, but also a two-week party that takes over the entire city (page 34).

◖ **Kentucky State Fair:** This annual August event draws people from all over the state to celebrate what makes Kentucky special, featuring everything from agricultural exhibits to arts and crafts competitions. Shows, concerts, midway rides, and more food than you can eat are all part of the tradition (page 37).

◖ **Olmsted Park System:** In a city full of green spaces, the parks designed by Frederick Law Olmsted stand out as hometown favorites. Follow the parkways from the open fields of Cherokee Park to the formal gardens of Shawnee Park to the forested hills of Iroquois Park (page 40).

© AVALON TRAVEL

LOOK FOR ◖ TO FIND RECOMMENDED SIGHTS, ACTIVITIES, DINING, AND LODGING.

transplant and first artificial heart transplant, more good restaurants than one could possibly hope to visit, and the headquarters of major corporations like Yum! Brands and UPS.

For others, their affection for Louisville relates to its small-town charm and its ability to maintain a strong identity even as the city grows. They love that the first question Louisvillians ask when they meet each other is "Where did you go to high school?", that the city supports its college sports teams with the same gusto as other cities support professional teams, that Heine Brothers is more popular than Starbucks, that downtown's golden-era hotels and Old Louisville's Victorian mansions are as revered as any new development, and that the best museums celebrate local goodness like the Louisville Slugger and Muhammad Ali.

As for what puts Louisville on the world's map—well, it's a little thing really, just a two-minute spectacle. Run every first Saturday in May, the Kentucky Derby and the accompanying two-week festival are the city's pride and joy and the state's largest tourism event. Put it on your calendar, because it's a spectacle that everyone should see at least once.

Whatever your tastes, Louisville will win you over. The old dame's no one-hit wonder, and her charm is guaranteed to bring you back time and again.

PLANNING YOUR TIME

Louisville tourism spikes in late April and early May, and for good reason. Many visitors plan their trips around the Kentucky Derby, which is always run on the first Saturday in May, and the Kentucky Derby Festival, which kicks off two weeks before Derby Day. It's a great time to visit. With a little luck, the weather is beautiful, with robin-egg blue skies, pleasantly warm days, and spring flowers painting the city with color. With everything spit-polished and shined, the city is prepared to win over the world. But beware, the weather doesn't always cooperate (both

© THERESA DOWELL BLACKINTON

Louisville's skyline, as seen from the Big 4 Bridge

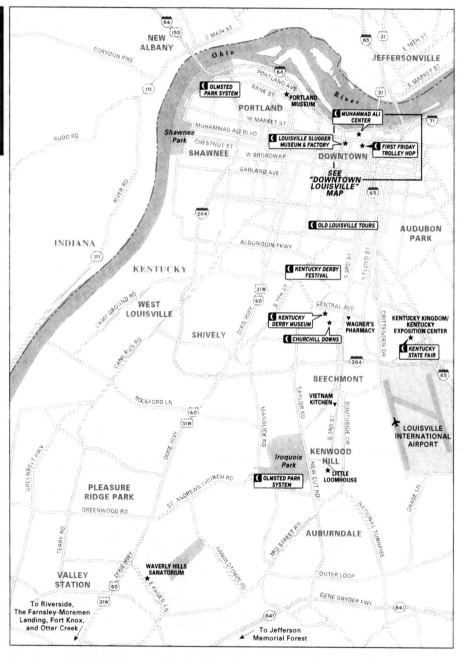

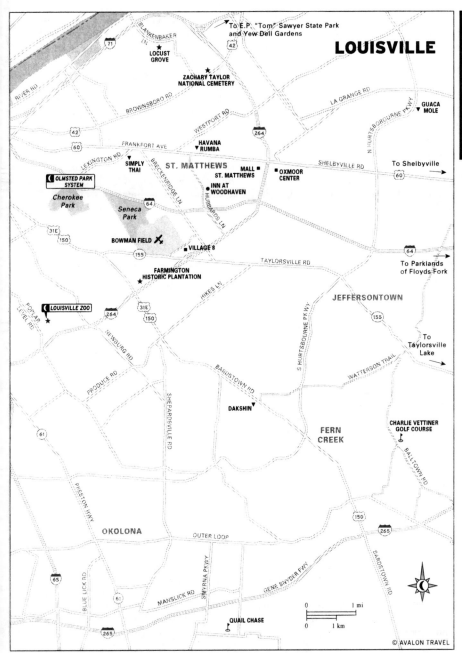

snowstorms and heat waves have been known to hit on Derby Day), hotel prices will be through the roof (if you can manage to secure a reservation at all), and restaurants will have long waits (show up well before you're hungry).

If you're not set on attending the Derby, choose another time to visit. Weather-wise, spring and fall are the most pleasant. Winters usually aren't too bad, although the city does get socked with a major storm every few years. Summers are hot and humid, but they're packed with things to do.

As for how long to stay, aim for a long weekend. You'll be able to cover most of the city's museums and sights all while enjoying leisurely meals at Louisville's fine restaurants as well as evenings out on the town. If you're interested in visiting any of the surrounding areas, such as Fort Knox or Shelbyville, tack an extra day onto your itinerary.

Most visitors will want to set themselves up in downtown or Old Louisville, where you'll find the city's best accommodations and restaurants as well as have easy access to most attractions. If you're looking to explore more of the state, Louisville makes an excellent jumping-off point, with day trips to Lexington, Frankfort, and the Bourbon Trail distilleries easy possibilities.

Sights

DOWNTOWN

Over the past two decades, Louisville's downtown has regained its title as the heart of the city. West Main Street's **Museum Row** (known as Whiskey Row in the early 1900s), stretching the four blocks from 5th to 9th Streets, can easily keep you busy for a weekend, if not a full week, and the **NuLu** area (New Louisville, or the East Market District) is the hot place to be these days, especially for eating, nightlife, and shopping. Adding oomph to the downtown experience is the city's notable architecture, as well as the lively waterfront scene.

If you plan to hit a lot of the museums, consider purchasing the **Main Ticket,** available online (www.gotolouisville.com/main-ticket) or at the **Louisville Visitors Center** (301 S. 4th St., 10am-5pm Mon.-Sat., noon-5pm Sun.). This ticket, which costs $29.99 for adults and $23.99 for youth 6-12, is good for one year and allows for admission to the Frazier International History Museum, the Louisville Slugger Museum & Factory, the Louisville Science Center, Kentucky Museum of Art & Craft, the Muhammad Ali Center, and KentuckyShow!

Frazier International History Museum

On the far western end of Museum Row, the **Frazier International History Museum** (829 W. Main St., 502/753-5663, www.fraziermuseum.org, 9am-5pm Mon.-Sat., noon-5pm Sun., $10.50 adults, $8.50 seniors, $7.50 students 14-17 and college students with ID, $6 youth 5-13) bears the honor of being the only place outside the United Kingdom to house a permanent exhibition of items from the Royal Armoury, the U.K.'s prized national collection of many centuries' worth of arms and armor. The museum's collections go far beyond the Armoury pieces, however, with Teddy Roosevelt's "Big Stick," Geronimo's bow, the Daniel Boone family bible, Lewis and Clark artifacts, and Frank and Jesse James's letters all finding homes at the Frazier. As impressive as the collections are, for many visitors they're overshadowed by the museum's 80 historical interpretations performed by a full-time staff of actor-historians. The 1,000-plus years of history on display at the Frazier come to life as Annie Oakley, Abraham Lincoln, Joan of Arc, and other historical figures make appearances

JUST ACROSS THE BRIDGE: INDIANA SIGHTS

Cross the Ohio River, and you'll find yourself in southern Indiana, which is for all intents and purposes a suburb of Louisville. A handful of interesting sights make a trip across the state line worthwhile.

Falls of the Ohio State Park & Interpretive Center (201 Riverside Dr., Clarksville, IN, 812/280-9970, www.fallsoftheohio.org, 9am-5pm Mon.-Sat., 1pm-5pm Sun., $5 adults, $2 youth) welcomes visitors to wander among 386-million-year-old fossil beds and search the 220 acres for signs of life from the Devonian period. The Interpretive Center hosts 100 different exhibits focusing on paleontology, geology, and history. A 14-minute movie, aquarium with fish found in the Ohio River, and a full-size mammoth skeleton are visitor favorites. If you just want to wander among the fossils or have a picnic at the river's edge, the park itself is open 7am-11pm, and you must pay a $2 parking fee.

Enjoy a night out at **Derby Dinner Playhouse** (525 Marriott Dr., Clarksville, IN, 812/288-8281, www.derbydinner.com), a dinner theater that specializes in productions of Broadway musicals, having put on all 50 of the top musicals of all time. There are no bad seats at the in-the-square theater, and a vocal ensemble entertains you as you enjoy your buffet dinner. Performances are held Tuesday-Sunday evenings with matinees on Wednesday and Sunday. Ticket prices range $35-44.

The **Howard Steamboat Museum** (1101 E. Market St., Jeffersonville, IN, 812/283-3728, www.steamboatmuseum.org, 10am-4pm Tues.-Sat., 1pm-4pm Sun., $6 adults, $5 seniors, $3.50 students) invites you to return to the golden era of steamboat travel on a tour through the 1894 mansion of the steamboat magnate Howard family. Models of steamboats, photographs, and artifacts are found throughout the grand house.

The **Carnegie Center for Art & History** (201 E. Spring St., New Albany, IN, 812/944-7336, www.carnegiecenter.org, 10am-5:30pm Tues.-Sat., free) features an award-winning exhibit on the Underground Railroad as well as a smile-inducing collection of hand-carved, mechanized dioramas depicting rural life at the end of the 19th century. Each year the center also hosts a juried art quilt exhibition, drawing entries from contemporary fiber artists across the country.

A visit to **Huber's Orchard, Winery & Vineyards** (19816 Huber Rd., Starlight, IN, 812/923-9463, www.huberwinery.com, 10am-6pm Mon.-Sat., noon-6pm Sun., extended hours May-Oct.) is an annual tradition for many locals, especially during apple- and pumpkin-picking seasons. Year-round you can take a complimentary wine tour with tasting (11am, 2pm, and 4pm Mon.-Sat., 2pm and 4pm Sun.), purchase produce at the farm market, and enjoy a hearty farm meal at the Starlight Café. A Farm Park ($6) with mountain slides, pedal karts, rope mazes, and mini-tractor rides welcomes kids.

on the 1st floor stage or in the 3rd floor Tournament Ring.

⚓ Louisville Slugger Museum & Factory

Louisville might not have a Major League Baseball team, but America's pastime wouldn't be the same if it weren't for the Louisville Slugger, the official baseball bat of MLB. On a tour of the **Louisville Slugger Museum & Factory** (800 W. Main St., 877/775-8443, www.sluggermuseum.org, 9am-5pm Mon.-Sat., 11am-5pm Sun., $12 adults, $11 seniors, $7 youth 6-12), visitors can learn how the history of baseball and the Louisville Slugger go hand in hand, take a practice swing with bats used by favorite players of the past and present, and tour the factory where each bat is made with as much love and care as in 1884, the year the Louisville Slugger was born. At the end of the tour, each participant receives a free miniature Louisville Slugger. Take it home with you

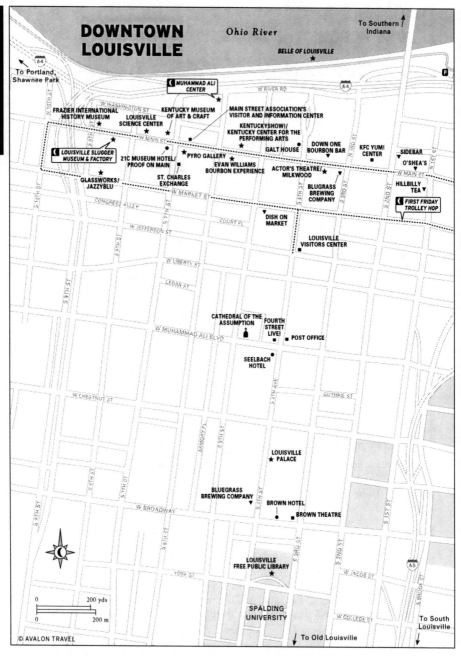

DOWNTOWN LOUISVILLE

Ohio River

To Southern Indiana

BELLE OF LOUISVILLE

To Portland, Shawnee Park

MUHAMMAD ALI CENTER

W RIVER RD

FRAZIER INTERNATIONAL HISTORY MUSEUM

KENTUCKY MUSEUM OF ART & CRAFT

MAIN STREET ASSOCIATION'S VISITOR AND INFORMATION CENTER

LOUISVILLE SCIENCE CENTER

KENTUCKYSHOW!/ KENTUCKY CENTER FOR THE PERFORMING ARTS

LOUISVILLE SLUGGER MUSEUM & FACTORY

21C MUSEUM HOTEL/ PROOF ON MAIN

PYRO GALLERY

GALT HOUSE

DOWN ONE BOURBON BAR

KFC YUM! CENTER

SIDEBAR

O'SHEA'S

EVAN WILLIAMS BOURBON EXPERIENCE

ST. CHARLES EXCHANGE

ACTOR'S THEATRE/ MILKWOOD

GLASSWORKS/ JAZZYBLU

HILLBILLY TEA

BLUGRASS BREWING COMPANY

FIRST FRIDAY TROLLEY HOP

CONGRESS ALLEY

W MARKET ST

DISH ON MARKET

W JEFFERSON ST

COURT PL

LOUISVILLE VISITORS CENTER

W LIBERTY ST

CEDAR ST

CATHEDRAL OF THE ASSUMPTION

FOURTH STREET LIVE!

W MUHAMMAD ALI BLVD

POST OFFICE

SEELBACH HOTEL

W CHESTNUT ST

GUTHRIE ST

LOUISVILLE PALACE

BLUEGRASS BREWING COMPANY

BROWN HOTEL

W BROADWAY

BROWN THEATRE

LOUISVILLE FREE PUBLIC LIBRARY

W JACOB ST

0   200 yds
0   200 m

SPALDING UNIVERSITY

W COLLEGE ST

To South Louisville

To Old Louisville

© AVALON TRAVEL

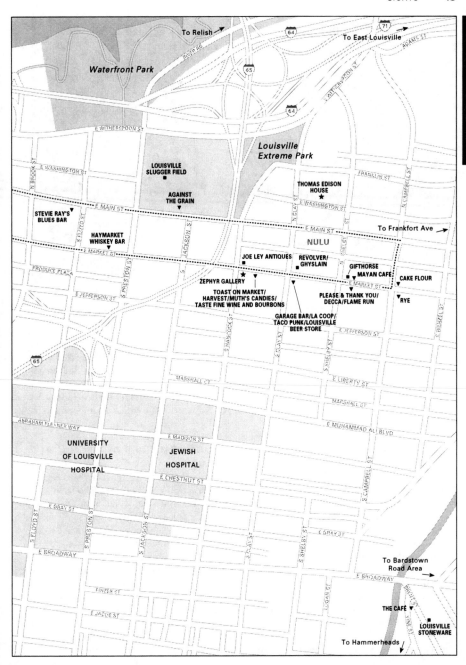

© THERESA DOWELL BLACKINTON

It takes more than two sets of arms to encircle the bat at the Louisville Slugger Museum.

(though only in your checked luggage!) after first posing with it in front of the world's largest bat, a 120-foot-tall, 68,000-pound steel replica of a Babe Ruth bat that greets everyone walking past the museum.

Louisville Science Center

More than a field-trip destination where you can see a mummy and be enclosed in a bubble, the **Louisville Science Center** (727 W. Main St., 800/591-2203, www.louisvillescience.org, 9:30am-5pm Sun.-Thurs., 9:30am-9pm Fri.-Sat., $13 adults, $11 youth 2-12) is an all-ages destination where science education meets hands-on fun. For the little ones under age seven, KidZone offers age-appropriate excitement, including exploration of occupations via dress-up and a table of wet and wild construction fun. Older children will enjoy the more than 150 learning stations in the museum's three permanent exhibitions—The World We Create, The World Within Us, and The World Around Us. The crawl-through cave and climb-aboard Gemini trainer space capsule are just a

few of the favorites that encourage visitors to engage with the exhibits. Special exhibitions are rolled out every 3-4 months and often appeal to adults, as do many of the standing exhibits, such as the ones on healthy living. An IMAX theater ($7) with a four-story screen completes the museum.

Kentucky Museum of Art & Craft

In a restored cast-iron building with cork floors and exposed beams, the **Kentucky Museum of Art & Craft** (715 W. Main St., 502/589-0102, www.kentuckyarts.org, 10am-5pm Tues.-Sat., 11am-5pm Sun., $8 adults, $5 seniors, $4 youth 13-17 and college students, $2 youth 6-12) celebrates the wealth of artistic talent and creativity found throughout the state. The museum's three galleries offer permanent and rotating exhibits featuring woodwork, textiles, ceramics, jewelry, photography, painting, and more. You'll likely find something you've never seen anywhere else and just have to have. Lucky for you, some items on display are also for sale, and there's a gift shop next to the galleries.

21C Museum

Occupying the reception area and lower atrium of the hotel of the same name, the **21C Museum** (700 W. Main St., 502/217-6300, www.21cmuseum.org, free) exhibits cutting-edge artwork from living artists. Exhibits change every six months, and the museum also offers a full program of film screenings, poetry readings, artist talks, and concert series. Pop in often, and don't forget to check out the elevator lobby as well as the restrooms—art isn't restricted to the galleries here; it's an integral part of the entire building.

◖ Muhammad Ali Center

While most museums beg you to keep your hands off the exhibits, the **Muhammad Ali Center** (144 N. 6th St., 502/584-9254, www.alicenter.org, 9:30am-5pm Tues.-Sat., noon-5pm Sun., $9 adults, $8 seniors, $5 students, $4 youth 6-12) repeatedly asks you to "Please touch." This hands-on, full-sensory, multimedia-heavy museum is a look at the life and times of The Greatest, a tribute to a hometown hero who became a universal icon. Far from one-sided, the Center depicts Ali the boxer, Ali the poet, and Ali the humanitarian, and it doesn't shy away from controversy, depicting Ali's losses alongside his wins, his radical comments alongside his inspirational quotes, his contentious choices alongside his universally celebrated moments. On the three floors of exhibition space, you can view a five-screen orientation film, test your boxing skills with punching bags and in a shadowboxing ring, watch your choice of Ali's 15 most famous fights, and check out memorabilia from Ali's life and career.

Evan Williams Bourbon Experience

When it opened in early 2014, the **Evan Williams Bourbon Experience** (528 W. Main St., 502/585-3923, www.evanwilliamsbourbonexperience.com, 10am-5pm Mon.-Sat., 1pm-5pm Sun.) became the first official Bourbon Trail site to be located in Louisville. Honoring Evan Williams, Kentucky's first distiller, and located in a Whiskey Row building across the street from the 18th-century Evan Williams distillery, the Experience immerses visitors in bourbon history, taking them back to 1783 on a guided tour through this artisanal distillery with museum-style exhibits. A tasting is included with the tour ($12 adults 21 and over, $9 youth 10-20).

KentuckyShow!

Want to get a taste of everything the great state of Kentucky has to offer before you dive into any deeper exploration? Then grab a seat at **KentuckyShow!** (501 W. Main St., 502/562-7800, www.kentuckyshow.com, $7 adults, $5 seniors and youth), a 30-minute multimedia production shown at the Kentucky Center for the Arts. Narrated by Kentuckian Ashley Judd, KentuckyShow! provides a moving look at Kentucky's history and culture, defining what makes the Bluegrass State such a special place. Screenings are offered on the hour 11am-4pm Tuesday-Saturday and 1pm-4pm Sunday.

Thomas Edison House

Before he invented the lightbulb, Thomas Edison was a Western Union telegraph operator in Louisville. The small four-room boarding house where he lived during that period, 1866-1867, is now the **Thomas Edison House** (729 E. Washington St., 502/585-5247, www.edisonhouse.org, 10am-2pm Tues.-Sat., $5 adults, $4 seniors, $3 youth 6-17). On a short tour of the property, visitors see his re-created room and can take a close look at a number of his inventions, including a working telegraph and phonograph.

Riverboat Cruises

The oldest river steamboat in operation, the *Belle of Louisville* (401 W. River Rd., 502/574-2992, www.belleoflouisville.org, May-Oct.) is both a National Landmark and a local icon. Using her big red paddlewheel, the *Belle* carries passengers up and down the Ohio River offering exceptional city views, all to the tune of her distinctive calliope. The Belle's sister boat, the *Spirit of Jefferson,* is a newer and

LOUISVILLE

© THERESA DOWELL BLACKINTON

boarding the *Belle of Louisville* for a cruise

smaller riverboat with modern conveniences. See the *Belle of Louisville* website for schedules for both boats, as well as information on special event cruises. Price depends on the type of cruise chosen, with options for lunch, dinner, sightseeing only, history, and moonlight tours.

Notable Architecture

Louisville's **West Main Street** is second only to New York City's SoHo in the number of cast-iron facade buildings. The eight-block area is also home to Greek Revival, Italianate, Richardsonian Romanesque, international, and postmodern architecture. Pick up a Walking Tour brochure from the **Main Street Association's Visitor and Information Center** (627 W. Main St., 502/589-6008, www.mainstreetassociation.com, 11am-3pm Mon.-Fri.) and explore the history and style that makes this one of Louisville's most architecturally interesting areas. Highlights include Mies van der Rohe's "rusted" **American Life and Accident Building** (3 Riverfront Plaza), Michael Graves's postmodern **Humana Building** (500 W. Main

St.), and the abundance of cast-iron buildings in the 600 and 700 blocks of West Main.

The gothic revival **Cathedral of the Assumption** (433 S. 5th St., 502/582-2971, www.cathedraloftheassumption.org) is the home of the Archdiocese of Louisville and a downtown landmark. Built in 1852, the cathedral was completely renovated in 1994. It boasts one of the oldest American-made stained-glass windows as well as a beautiful starred ceiling complete with restored fresco.

The collections at the **main branch of the Louisville Free Public Library** (301 York St., 502/574-1611, www.lfpl.org, 9am-9pm Mon.-Thurs., 9am-5pm Fri.-Sat., 2pm-5pm Sun.) are not limited to books and magazines, but also include photos and artifacts related to local history. Even if you're not a bibliophile, the library is worth a visit for a look at the South Building. Built in 1906 with funds from Andrew Carnegie, the beaux arts building features Ionic columns, ornamental friezes, marble floors, bronze doors, and large-scale mosaics and paintings.

PORTLAND

Located a bit west of downtown at the Falls of the Ohio, the current neighborhood of Portland was once an independent town and an important stop for riverboat traffic. Though the area has seen some hard times in the past decades, many Louisville old-timers have fond memories of Portland, and notable Louisvillians such as football great Paul Hornung grew up in the neighborhood.

Portland Museum

The **Portland Museum** (2308 Portland Ave., 502/776-7678, www.goportland.org, 10am-4:30pm Tues.-Thurs., $7 adults, $6 seniors, $5 students) explores the history of the land, river, and people who called Portland home and helped turn Louisville from a shipping port into a city. A light-and-sound-enhanced exhibit with detailed dioramas and lifelike human models tells the story of Portland, while additional galleries host rotating exhibits that illuminate life in this vibrant and historic district.

OLD LOUISVILLE

Home to the largest collection of Victorian mansions in the United States and showcasing a variety of impressive architectural styles of the late 19th and early 20th centuries, Old Louisville is a spirited neighborhood rich in history and perfect for on-foot exploration. It's also where you'll find the University of Louisville, which helps keep this old neighborhood young, hip, and richly diverse.

◖ Old Louisville Tours

To get the most out of a visit to Old Louisville, consider a tour. Do-it-yourselfers can choose from five self-guided walking/driving tours outlined in brochures produced by the **Old Louisville Visitors Center** (1217 S. 4th St., 502/637-2922, www.oldlouisville.org, 10am-4pm Tues.-Sat.). Those looking for a real insider's view should sign up for one of the outings with **Louisville Historic Tours** (502/637-2922, www.louisvillehistorictours.com), which employs neighborhood residents as guides. Guided walking tours include the

Old Louisville Grand Walking Tour (11am and 3pm Tues.-Sat., $15), the Old Louisville Ghost Walk (1pm Tues.-Thurs. and Sat., $20), and the Lantern Ghost Walk (7pm daily, $25). Guided bus tours include the Mansions & Milestones Tour (2:30pm Fri.-Sat., $25) and the Ghosts of Old Louisville Tour (7:30pm Fri., $25). Tours depart from the Old Louisville Visitors Center and last 1.5-2 hours. Reservations are recommended. For a chance to peek inside some of the neighborhood beauties, put the Holiday House Tour (www.oldlouisvilleholidayhometour.org, $30), held annually on the first weekend of December, on your calendar. The Hidden Treasure Garden Tour (www.oldlouisvillegardentour.com, $15), held annually in early July, offers a look at what's behind the wrought-iron fences of many neighborhood homes.

Conrad-Caldwell House

Of the many historic homes in Louisville, the **Conrad-Caldwell House** (1402 St. James Ct., 502/636-5023, www.conradcaldwell.org, $10 adults, $6 seniors, $4 students), a grand three-story Victorian mansion from the 1890s, might just be the most interesting to tour (1pm and 3pm Wed.-Sun., additional tour 11am Sat.). Named for Theophilus Conrad, who built and occupied the house for its first 10 years, and the William E. Caldwell family, who lived in the house through the 1920s, the house boasts beautiful parquet floors patterned after quilts; a remarkable attention to detail in the woodworked walls, staircases, and decorative features; and original furniture, books, and belongings from the Caldwell family. If you're lucky, you'll be guided through the house by a direct descendant of William Caldwell, bursting with intimate knowledge of the family and great stories about the house.

Crane House

Since 1987, **Crane House** (1244 S. 3rd St., 502/635-2240, www.cranehouse.org, 9:30am-4:30pm, Mon., Tues., Thurs., and Fri.) has been exposing Louisville residents and visitors to the culture of East Asia through a variety

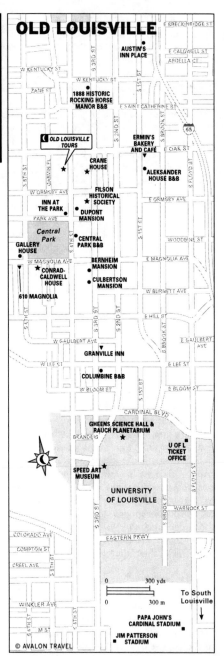

OLD LOUISVILLE

of programming. Visitors are welcome to take a free tour of Crane House, which includes a visit to the Asia Gallery, an exhibit of contemporary and historical Asian artifacts, as well as an introduction to Chinese tea and tea drinking. Crane House also offers Chinese cooking classes, Chinese and Japanese language classes, and Tai Chi classes. A regular lecture series is free and open to the public; check the online calendar.

Filson Historical Society

Home to extensive library collections chronicling local and Southern history, the **Filson Historical Society** (1310 S. 3rd St., 502/635-5083, www.filsonhistorical.org, 9am-4:30pm Mon.-Fri., free) is a gem for researchers. The excellent lecture series is also a boon to the community. Visit the website for a schedule of events. The Ferguson Mansion, home of the society, is worth a visit on its own merit. A self-guided tour describes the luxurious elements that made this beaux arts mansion the most expensive house in the city when it was built in 1905 and also allows visitors to view many of the society's artifacts, including a carving done by Daniel Boone, Civil War uniforms, a moonshine still, antique quilts, and a strong art collection.

University of Louisville

The **University of Louisville,** a public university, bustles with the energy of more than 21,000 students who come from around the state, country, and world to study in more than 170 fields. The urban campus isn't just for students, however; it also offers much to the community. Go ahead and take a stroll on the manicured grounds of Belknap Campus. You'll want to keep an eye out for one of the original casts of Rodin's *The Thinker,* which sits eternally lost in thought in front of the main administrative building, as well as the grave of U.S. Supreme Court Justice Louis Brandeis, which can be found under the portico of the law school that bears his name.

One of the most visited on-campus sites by the public is the **Speed Art Museum** (2035

the Conrad-Caldwell House

© THERESA DOWELL BLACKINTON

S. 3rd St., http://speedmuseum.org), home to Louisville's best art collection, with more than 13,000 works spanning 6,000 years. At the time of research, it was undergoing a three-year renovation and is scheduled to reopen in 2016. Check the website for updated information.

The nearby **Gheens Science Hall & Rauch Planetarium** (108 W. Brandeis Ave., 502/852-6664, www.louisville.edu/planetarium, $8 adults, $6 seniors and youth 12 and under) exposes the public to the wonders of space through a wide range of shows illuminating the night sky, the planets, our solar system, and far beyond. Locals might particularly enjoy the seasonal Skies over Louisville program, which explains exactly what it is you're seeing in the sky right over your own backyard. Also popular are the laser shows, which are set to tunes of the Beatles, Led Zeppelin, Radiohead, and other popular bands. Shows are generally offered at 8pm, 9pm, 10pm, and 11pm Friday; 1pm, 2pm, and 3pm Saturday; and 11am and noon Sunday. Check the website for complete show listings.

SOUTH LOUISVILLE

South Louisville has had a bit of a roller-coaster existence, soaring in the late 19th and first half of the 20th centuries as Churchill Downs and Iroquois Park laid claim to the area and a railcar line made the connection to downtown simple, then falling in the late 1900s as the factories that employed many of the area's middle-class workers left town. Now, this area, once a summer retreat and still the location of some of the city's most historic sites and homes, is again on the way up. A favorite area for new immigrants, South Louisville mixes local tradition with newly introduced customs.

Kentucky Kingdom

It's been a bumpy ride for **Kentucky Kingdom** (Crittenden Dr., Kentucky Exposition Center, www.kentuckykingdom.com, 11am-7pm Sun.-Fri. and 11am-9pm Sat. late May-mid-Aug, 5pm-9pm Mon.-Fri. and 12pm-9pm Sat.-Sun. mid-late Aug., 11am-7pm Mon., Sat., and Sun. Sept., $44.95 general admission, $34.95 children under 48 inches and seniors, $8 parking), the local amusement park, since it was dropped by Six Flags in 2010. However, Kentucky Kingdom finally has new owners, and will reopen on May 24, 2014, with new and longtime favorite rides, a dedicated kids' area, and an expanded Hurricane Bay waterpark. Season passes ($59.95) are a great deal for those planning to visit the park more than once.

◖ Kentucky Derby Museum and Churchill Downs

If you can't make it to the Derby, experiencing the thrill of the most exciting two minutes in sports on the 360-degree high-definition screen at the **Kentucky Derby Museum** (704 Central Ave., 502/637-7097, www.derbymuseum.org, 8am-5pm Mon.-Sat., 11am-5pm Sun., Mar. 15-Nov., 9am-5pm Mon.-Sat., 11am-5pm Sun., Dec.-Mar. 14, $14 adults, $13 seniors, $11 youth 13-18, $6 youth 5-12) is the next best thing. In addition to the film, interactive exhibits and authentic artifacts allow you to get a taste of Derby Day, discover what it takes to create a champion thoroughbred, and learn about the pursuit of victory from the perspective of jockey, trainer, and owner. The museum was damaged extensively by flooding in early 2009, and while closed for recovery, museum exhibits were overhauled and updated. Your admission ticket also allows you to take a guided walking tour of **Churchill Downs,** the racetrack where the Derby is run every May under the famed twin spires. For a more in-depth look at the historic track, the museum also offers an Inside the Gates Walking Tour ($11), a Barn & Backside Van Tour ($11), a Twilight Tour (3rd Thurs. of the month, $15), and a Horses & Haunts Tour (Oct. only, $15).

THE BIRTH OF THE HAPPY BIRTHDAY SONG

There are some things that seem as if they've simply always existed—the Happy Birthday song being a fine example. Sung to us annually by friends and family to mark the passing of another year, and memorably spiced up by Marilyn Monroe for President Kennedy, "Happy Birthday to You" is so omnipresent in our society that healthcare officials even suggest we sing it as we wash our hands to ensure that we scrub for the proper amount of time needed to kill germs.

But once upon a time, not long before the 19th century turned to the 20th, the Happy Birthday song did not exist. How they celebrated birthdays then, heaven knows, but apparently they did still have parties, because it was at a birthday celebration on what is now the Little Loomhouse property in South Louisville that sisters Patty and Mildred J. Hill introduced the song for the first time. Both kindergarten teachers, the sisters had originally written a song in 1893 called "Good Morning to All," which was well loved by their students. By keeping the melody but changing the simple lyrics, the Hill sisters created history and made birthdays better for all of us.

Little Loomhouse

Preserving the legacy of Lou Tate, a master weaver whose work was admired by the likes of first ladies Eleanor Roosevelt and Lou Hoover, the **Little Loomhouse** (328 Kenwood Hill Rd., 502/367-4792, www.littleloomhouse. org, 10am-3:30pm Tues.-Thurs. and 3rd Sat. of the month, $5) offers tours of her home and workshop. You'll set foot in the cabin where "Happy Birthday" was first sung, see samples of the intricate patterns Lou Tate helped preserve, and learn to weave on a little loom. More in-depth weaving classes are offered in multiweek sessions. The gift shop sells a guidebook to the surrounding neighborhood that will allow you to better explore the area.

Waverly Hills Sanatorium

If your idea of a good time is having the living daylights scared out of you, then add **Waverly Hills Sanatorium** (4400 Paralee Ln., 502/933-2142, www.therealwaverlyhills.com) to your must-see list. This former tuberculosis health care facility and geriatric center is said to be one of the most haunted sites in the United States. For those brave enough, the sanatorium offers half-night (midnight-4am Fri., Mar.-Aug., $50) and full-night (midnight-8am Sat., Mar.-Aug., $100) paranormal investigations that are said to have turned up sightings of ghosts, ectoplasm clouds, and lights where there is no electricity, as well as the sounds of voices, cries, screams, slamming doors, and bouncing balls. A shorter two-hour tour is also available (Fri. and Sat., Mar.-Aug., $22). If just reading this makes you want to hide under a blanket, then opt for the two-hour historical tour (2:30pm Sun., Mar.-Aug., 8pm Wed., Sept.-Oct., $22). All tours must be reserved in advance and are often booked months ahead. Proceeds fund the restoration of the building.

Riverside, The Farnsley-Moremen Landing

Experience life at a 19th-century Ohio River farm on a visit to **Riverside, The Farnsley-Moremen Landing** (7410 Moorman Rd., 502/935-6809, www.riverside-landing.org,

© THERESA DOWELL BLACKINTON

A horse races at Churchill Downs.

10am-4:30pm Tues.-Sat., year-round, 1pm-4:30pm Sun., Mar.-Nov. only, final tour at 3:30, $6 adults, $5 seniors, $3 youth 6-12), a popular stop for boat traffic back when the river was equivalent to today's interstate. A tour will take you into the house, remarkable for its two-story Greek Revival portico. You'll notice that it's decorated in two different styles: the first floor re-creates life in 1840 when Gabriel Farnsley lived in the house as a bachelor; the second draws its style from 1880 when three generations of the Moremen family occupied the house. You'll also visit the detached kitchen, as well as the kitchen garden, where volunteers grow plants that very likely would have been served at mealtime in the 1800s. Be sure to enjoy the view of the river from the grounds; it's photo worthy.

FRANKFORT AVENUE AND EAST LOUISVILLE

Frankfort Avenue, running east from downtown, is a lively neighborhood known more for its restaurants and shopping than its attractions, though it's easy to spend a day exploring the area and enjoying the ambience. Once the gateway between Frankfort (hence the name) and Louisville, Frankfort Avenue is chockablock with historic buildings that have maintained their style despite finding new uses. Continuing east from Frankfort Avenue, you'll find yourself in East Louisville, a popular residential area that also houses interesting sights, primarily historical. With amorphous boundaries—you'll get a lot of different answers if you ask a local just what East Louisville includes—the sights in this section are located as close as 5 minutes and as distant as 30 minutes from downtown.

American Printing House for the Blind

The museum of the **American Printing House for the Blind** (1839 Frankfort Ave., 502/895-2405, www.aph.org, 8:30am-4:30pm Mon.-Fri., 10am-3pm Sat., free), the oldest and largest producer of materials for the visually impaired, features hands-on

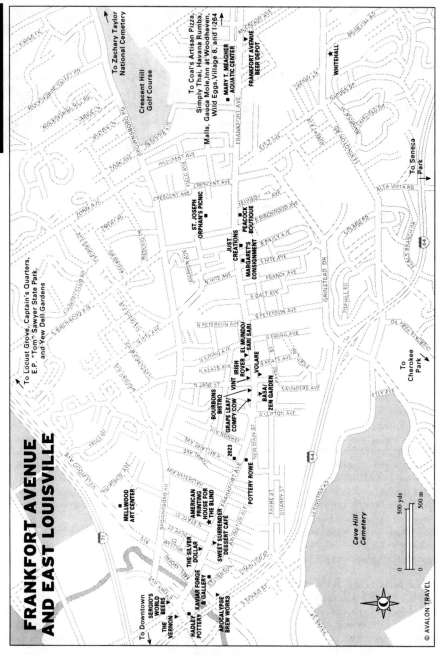

FRANKFORT AVENUE AND EAST LOUISVILLE

© AVALON TRAVEL

exhibits that document the evolution of tactile reading systems for the blind, and contains items such as a 142-volume Braille translation of an encyclopedia, a Braille bible used by Helen Keller, and a variety of Braille typewriters you can try. For a more in-depth look at the fascinating work done by the APH, take a free tour (10am and 2pm Mon.-Thurs.), where you'll get to see the printing press in action and listen in on the recording of Talking Books.

Whitehall

Although it began its life as a modest red-brick Italianate farmhouse, **Whitehall** (3110 Lexington Rd., 502/897-2944, www.historichomes.org, 10am-2pm Mon.-Fri., $5 adults, $4 seniors, $3 youth 6-18) grew from its humble 1855 origins to become an imposing Southern-style Greek Revival mansion. On a tour of its 15 rooms, you'll learn the history of the home and see the elaborate stylings introduced by the home's two most prominent owners. The Middleton family, who bought the house in 1909, renovated it into the style we see today, while the Hume family, who occupied the house from 1924 to 1992, made the necessary arrangements for Whitehall to become a historic property. Intricate fireplaces and wood floors, period wallpaper, and beautifully carved furniture imported from around the world give Whitehall its sumptuous feel. Don't forget to check out the gorgeous gardens, which can be visited for free dawn-dusk.

Zachary Taylor National Cemetery

Originally the family burial grounds of the 12th President of the United States, **Zachary Taylor National Cemetery** (4701 Brownsboro Rd., 502/893-3852, www.cem.va.gov, sunrise-sunset daily) was given federal status in 1928, 78 years after Old Rough and Ready was laid to rest. Now joining President Taylor and his family in eternal rest are U.S. military members who served the nation in the years ranging from the Spanish-American War to the

Locust Grove

Persian Gulf War. A life-size statue atop a 50-foot granite monument marks the grave of the Kentuckian president.

Locust Grove

Visited by three presidents as well as the returning Lewis and Clark, and lived in by Louisville founder George Rogers Clark for the last nine years of his life, **Locust Grove** (561 Blankenbaker Ln., 502/897-9845, www.locustgrove.org, 10am-4:30pm Mon.-Sat., 1pm-4:30pm Sun., last tour at 3:15pm, $8 adults, $7 seniors, $4 youth 6-12) has played host to more than its share of history. Now this carefully restored 18th-century Georgian mansion, its grounds, formal gardens, and outbuildings are open to the public. A visit begins with a short film at a quarter past the hour and then moves on to a 45-minute tour of the property, followed by a chance to explore the museum. You'll learn about early Kentucky history, westward expansion, frontier life, and slave life all while enjoying the beautiful setting. Each December, special holiday candlelight tours are offered, giving visitors a taste of an old-fashioned Christmas.

Yew Dell Gardens

Recognized by the Garden Conservancy for its exceptional nature, **Yew Dell Gardens** (6220 Old Lagrange Rd., Crestwood, 502/241-4788, www.yewdellgardens.org, 10am-4pm Tues.-Sat., noon-4pm Sun., Apr.-mid-Dec., 10am-4pm Mon.-Fri., mid-Dec.-Mar., $7 adults, $5 seniors, free youth under 12) is 33 acres of bliss for anyone who loves plants and remarkable landscaping. The once private gardens of renowned horticulturist Theodore Klein, who died in 1998, opened to the public in 2005. Visitors can now marvel at the more than 1,000 specimens of rare trees and shrubs in his arboretum and explore a variety of themed gardens. Favorites include the Secret Garden, the formal Topiary Garden, the English Walled Garden, the summertime Bloom Garden, and the evergreen Serpentine Garden.

BARDSTOWN ROAD AREA

For many residents of Louisville, Bardstown Road, which runs south from downtown toward the suburbs, perfectly sums up the Derby City. As with Frankfort Avenue, Bardstown Road is a happening hub that, despite not having too many tourist attractions per se, is a place where you could easily pass an entire day. It's the place to experience a Louisvillian's Louisville.

Cave Hill Cemetery

Cave Hill Cemetery (701 Baxter Ave., 502/451-5630, www.cavehillcemetery.com, 8am-4:45pm daily) is not just a burial ground; it's also an arboretum, a masterpiece of landscape architecture, and a sculpture park. While strolling the grounds, you can admire the artwork adorning graves, identify more than 500 species of tree and shrub, and feed the waterfowl that live on the lake. Don't forget to pay your respects to Colonel Sanders (section 33, marked with a bust) and other Kentucky notables such as city founder George Rogers Clark (section P). In the spring and fall, historical and geological tours are offered; visit the website for dates and fees.

Farmington Historic Plantation

Farmington (3033 Bardstown Rd., 502/452-9920, www.historichomes.org, 10am-4pm Tues.-Fri., $9 adults, $8 seniors, $4 youth 6-18), the Federal-style home that sits at the heart of a former hemp plantation owned by the venerable Speed family, gives visitors a peek into genteel life in the early 1800s. Known for their philanthropic giving around Louisville, the Speed family had ties to both Thomas Jefferson and Abraham Lincoln, and Farmington gives special attention to the family's relationship with the latter. A permanent exhibition explores what life was like at Farmington when Lincoln spent three weeks there in 1841 and details Lincoln's relationships with Joshua Speed, whom he called his "most intimate friend," and James Speed, who served as Lincoln's attorney general. Another

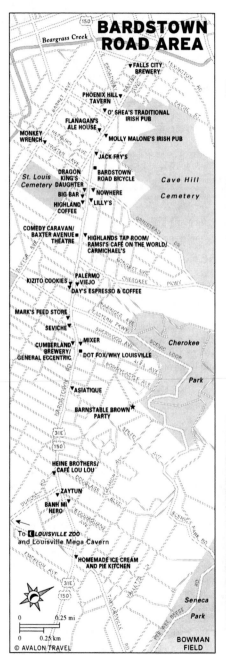

BARDSTOWN ROAD AREA

Beargrass Creek

FALLS CITY BREWERY
PHOENIX HILL TAVERN
O' SHEA'S TRADITIONAL IRISH PUB
FLANAGAN'S ALE HOUSE
MONKEY WRENCH
MOLLY MALONE'S IRISH PUB
JACK FRY'S
DRAGON KING'S DAUGHTER
BARDSTOWN ROAD BICYCLE
St. Louis Cemetery
BIG BAR
NOWHERE
HIGHLAND COFFEE
LILLY'S
Cave Hill Cemetery
COMEDY CARAVAN/ BAXTER AVENUE THEATRE
HIGHLANDS TAP ROOM/ RAMSI'S CAFE ON THE WORLD/ CARMICHAEL'S
KIZITO COOKIES
PALERMO VIEJO
DAY'S ESPRESSO & COFFEE
MARK'S FEED STORE
SEVICHE
CUMBERLAND BREWERY/ GENERAL ECCENTRIC
MIXER
DOT FOX/WHY LOUISVILLE
Cherokee
ASIATIQUE
Park
BARNSTABLE BROWN PARTY
HEINE BROTHERS/ CAFÉ LOU LOU
ZAYTUN
BANH MI HERO
To LOUISVILLE ZOO and Louisville Mega Cavern
HOMEMADE ICE CREAM AND PIE KITCHEN
Seneca Park
BOWMAN FIELD

0   0.25 mi
0   0.25 km
© AVALON TRAVEL

permanent exhibition details the lives of slaves at Farmington. Try to time your visit to coincide with one of their reenactments, which really bring history to life.

◖ Louisville Zoo

With its nationally recognized four-acre Gorilla Forest and its award-winning Glacier Run, which allows for underwater and aboveground viewing of polar bears, the **Louisville Zoo** (1100 Trevilian Way, 502/459-2181, www.louisvillezoo.org, 10am-4pm daily, Sep.-mid-Mar., 10am-5pm daily, mid-Mar.-Aug., $15.95 adults, $11.50 seniors and youth 3-11, $5 parking fee) is one of the best zoos in the country. Follow the simple loop layout to catch all 1,300 residents of the zoo, ranging from the tiny frogs of the Amazonian rainforest to the giant elephants of the African plains. Regularly scheduled training and feeding programs add to the experience, as do the natural settings and informational panels. Going beyond animals, the zoo hosts a few

© THERESA DOWELL BLACKINTON

giraffes at the Louisville Zoo

extremely popular events. August's **Brew at the Zoo** is a celebration of local and regional microbrews and good music that always sells out in advance. For kids, October's **World's Largest Halloween Party,** which features trick-or-treating around the decorated zoo, is a real treat.

Louisville Mega Cavern

Lying underneath the Louisville Zoo and much of the surrounding area, **Louisville Mega Cavern** (1841 Taylor Ave., 877/614-6342, www.louisvillemegacavern.com), which

was once a limestone quarry, is now a tourist spot. You can explore it on a one-hour historic tram tour (tours at 10am, noon, 2pm, and 4pm daily, mid-Jan.-mid-Mar., on the hour 10am-4pm daily, mid-Mar.-Memorial Day and Labor Day-Oct., on the hour 9am-5pm Mon.-Fri. and 9am-6pm Sat.-Sun., Memorial Day-Labor Day, $13.50 adults, $12 seniors, $8 youth 3-11) or on a two-hour tour via six underground zip lines (reserve online; $59-79). During the Christmas season, the cavern is decked out in holiday lights, which can be enjoyed on a self-drive tour.

Entertainment and Events

BARS AND CLUBS

Louisville has a happening bar and club scene that centers around three areas: downtown, Frankfort Avenue, and the Bardstown Road/Baxter Avenue corridor. Vibes range from neighborhood joint to upscale bar, so no matter your taste, you'll find something that's your style. While most cities go dark around 2am, Louisville is unique in that some nightlife locales don't shut down until 4am.

Downtown

Louisville's downtown has been undergoing a nightlife reawakening in the past decade, with the opening of the KFC Yum! Center in 2010 and the revitalization of the area known as NuLu further spurring it on. For those fond of tradition, a few longtime institutions have opened outposts downtown, including Irish pub **Patrick O' Shea's** (123 W. Main St., 502/708-2488, www.osheaslouisville.net, 11am-1am Mon.-Wed., 11am-4am Thurs.-Sat.) and **Bluegrass Brewing Company** (300 W. Main St., 502/562-0007, www.bbcbrew.com, 11am-midnight Mon.-Thurs., 11am-1am Fri.-Sat.), a well-loved microbrewery.

Additionally, multiple new establishments have flung open their doors, turning cool old buildings into hot new spots. From west to east, the following locales are worth checking out.

St. Charles Exchange (113 S. 7th St., 502/618-1917, http://stcharlesexchange.com, 4pm-midnight Mon.-Thurs., 4pm-2am Fri., 5pm-2am Sat., 5pm-10:30pm Sun.) serves top-notch cocktails as well as American wines, craft beers, and bourbons (plus a fine menu of contemporary American fare) from a long handsome bar on a black-and-white checked floor, giving it the feel of old-fashioned elegance. As one might expect, **Down One Bourbon Bar** (321 W. Main St., 502/566-3259, www.downonebourbonbar.com, 11am-11pm Mon.-Thurs., 11am-1am Fri., 4pm-1am Sat.) stocks an impressive array of bourbons, to be sampled by the glass, in flights, or in a cocktail, but they also have a fine beer list as well as wines and non-bourbon cocktails. Another bourbon-based hot spot is **Sidebar** (129 N. 2nd St., 502/384-1600, www.sidebarwhiskeyrow.com, 11am-1am Mon.-Wed., 11am-2am Thurs.-Sat., noon-1am Sun.), which is fittingly located in a loft in Louisville's old Whiskey Row; try one of the aged cocktails or ask the knowledgeable bartenders for their picks. For some live music with your choice of drink (more than 50 whiskeys as well as bottled beers and seven craft beers on tap), try **Haymarket Whiskey Bar** (331 E. Market St., 502/442-0523, http://haymarketwhiskeybar.com, 4:20pm-midnight Tues.-Thurs., 4:20pm-2am Fri.-Sat.).

© THERESA DOWELL BLACKINTON

the NuLu neighborhood

Downtown's **Fourth Street Live!** (400 S. 4th St., www.4thstlive.com) likes to bill itself as the place to be, but to be honest, most locals aren't big fans of it. Besides **Maker's Mark Bourbon House & Lounge** (502/568-9009, www.makerslounge.com, 11am-11:30pm Mon.-Thurs., 11am-3am Fri.-Sat., 11am-midnight Sun.), where you can kick back in a leather chair and sip one of the more than 70 bourbons on offer, few of the bars have any sort of Louisville feel, and you're most likely to find tourists and frat boys hanging out here. If you do want to check it out, the other nightlife establishments here are **Kill Devil Club,** a cocktail bar open Thursday-Saturday nights; **Marquee Bar,** a dance club with table service open only on Friday and Saturday nights; and **PBR Louisville,** a cowboy-themed club open Thursday-Saturday nights.

Frankfort Avenue

In addition to multiple fine restaurant bars, Frankfort Avenue also boasts destinations where drinking is the focus. **The Vernon** (1575 Story Ave., 502/584-8460, www.vernonclub. com, 5pm-midnight Mon.-Tues., 5pm-1am Wed.-Thurs., 3pm-1am Fri., noon-1am Sat., 1pm-1am Sun.)—part club, part bowling alley with bar—has played a part in Louisville history since the late 1800s. The club hosts shows by up-and-coming bands (check the online schedule), and The Vernon's eight lanes are the coolest place in town to doff bowling shoes. For a change from the usual scene, The Vernon is your spot.

Sergio's World Beers (1605 Story Ave., 502/618-2337, www.sergiosworldbeers.com, 2pm-midnight Mon.-Thurs., 2pm-2am Fri.-Sat., 2pm-11pm Sun.) is not the place to go if you think that beer is beer. If, however, you are a discerning beer drinker, then you'll want to locate this discreet (there's no signage) temple to beer to surround yourself with like-minded individuals and get lost in the selection of 1,400 beers, more than 40 of which are on tap.

For bourbon fans, you'll want to head to one of two destinations. **Bourbons Bistro** (2255 Frankfort Ave., 502/894-8838, www.

LOUISVILLE'S CRAFT BEER SCENE

Louisville's contemporary craft beer scene dates back to the early 1990s, long before the country went mad for microbrews, but it's grown substantially in the past decade. Fans of local brews will want to check out the following microbreweries, some of which focus exclusively on beer while others have a restaurant element as well. True aficionados will want to be in Louisville in September for the nine-day **Louisville Craft Beer Week,** which features beer dinners, beer pairings, beer walks, brewery parties, and more at locations all around town.

AGAINST THE GRAIN

Located in the old train station at Louisville Slugger Field, **Against the Grain** (401 E. Main St., 502/515-0174, www.atgbrewery.com, 11pm-midnight Mon.-Wed., 11am-2am Thurs.-Sat., noon-9pm Sun.) brews beers in six broad categories—session, hop, whim, malt, dark, and smoke—with the particular beers on tap constantly rotating. The 15-copper-barrel brewhouse is also a smokehouse restaurant.

APOCALYPSE BREW WORKS

Opened in 2012, **Apocalypse Brew Works** (1612 Mellwood Ave., 502/589-4843, http://apocalypsebrewworks.com, 5pm-11pm Fri.-Sat.) is a homebrew operation that focuses on small-batch beers. Their beers run the gamut from stouts, porters, and IPAs to fruit and specialty beers. On their 10 taps, you might find Creamation, Atomic Amber, Apollo IPA, or Smokin Pyres Porter.

BLUEGRASS BREWING COMPANY

The oldest of Louisville's microbreweries and the largest microbrewery in Kentucky, **Bluegrass Brewing Company** (known locally as BBC) has been keeping Louisville in beer since 1993. They have three restaurant locations (http://bbcbrew.com; 3929 Shelbyville Rd., 502/899-7051, 11am-midnight Mon.-Thurs., 11am-1am Fri.-Sat., noon-10pm Sun.; 660 S. 4th St., 502/568-2224, 11am-midnight Mon.-Thurs., 11am-1am Fri.-Sat.; 300 W. Main St., 502/562-0007, 11am-midnight Mon.-Thurs., 11am-1am Fri.-Sat., 1pm-10pm Sun.) where you can try their American Pale Ale, Dark Star Porter, German Alt Beer, Nut Brown Ale, or Raspberry Mead, as well as rotating specials. Additionally, their **production brewery** (636 E. Main St., 502/584-2739, http://bluegrassbrew.com, 4pm-10pm Tues.-Fri.), which hosts a taproom and a museum of objects representing brewing history in Louisville, is also open to the public.

CUMBERLAND BREWERY

An integral part of the Bardstown Road scene, **Cumberland Brewery** (1576 Bardstown Rd., 502/458-8727, www.cumberlandbrewery.com, 4pm-2am Mon.-Thurs., noon-2am Fri.-Sat., 1pm-2am Sun.) keeps their regulars happy with their selection of cream ales, pale ales, porters, wheat ales, bocks, meades, and saisons, as well as their tasty menu of bar favorites.

FALLS CITY BREWERY

First opened in 1905, but then closed in 1978, **Falls City Brewery** (545 E. Barrett Ave., www.fallscitybeer.com, 4pm-8pm Thurs.-Fri., 2pm-8pm Sat.) was revived in 2010 as a craft brewery. Their first new beer after coming back onto the scene was an English pale ale. At the brewery and taproom, you can sample the goods or grab a growler to go.

NEW ALBANIAN BREWING COMPANY

Technically not in Louisville, but instead across the bridge in Indiana, **New Albanian Brewing Company** (www.newalbanian.com) has a hearty Louisville fan base. Since opening in 2002, New Albanian has brewed more than 30 beers, including Hoptimus, an imperial IPA; Black & Blue Grass, an ale spiced with lemongrass, black pepper, and agave; and Bob's Old 15B, a brown porter. The brews can be tried at their **pub and pizzeria** (3312 Plaza Dr., New Albany, IN, 812/944-2577, 11am-midnight Mon.-Sat.), from which you have a view of the R&D brewery, or at the **Bank Street Brewhouse** (415 Bank St., New Albany, IN, 812/725-9585, 11am-10pm Tues.-Thurs., 11am-11pm Fri.-Sat., 10am-9pm Sun.), a bistro-style restaurant where the production brewery is located.

bourbonsbistro.com, 5pm-10pm Tues.-Thurs., 5pm-11pm Fri.-Sat., 5pm-9pm Sun.) pours more than 130 bourbons, and also hosts bourbon dinners and other events in addition to serving a regular bourbon-based dinner menu. **The Silver Dollar** (1761 Frankfort Ave., 502/259-9540, www.whiskeybythe-drink.com, 5pm-2am daily), which has a bit of a honky-tonk feel and serves Southern-meets-Californian food, has a four-page bourbon list, a three-page beer list, and substantial numbers of whiskeys and tequilas.

Bardstown Road

Louisville's nightlife center for decades, Bardstown Road is still where many locals go to meet and mingle or just grab a stool at the neighborhood watering hole. Many a weekend gets kicked off at Louisville's Irish corner, located just past where Bardstown Road turns into Baxter Avenue. It's the home of **O'Shea's Traditional Irish Pub** (956 Baxter Ave., 502/589-7373, www.osheaslouisville. net, 4pm-2am Mon., 11am-2am Tues., 11am-4am Wed.-Sat.), **Flanagan's Ale House** (934 Baxter Ave., 502/585-3700, http://flanagansalehouse.com, 11am-2am Sun.-Wed., 11am-4am Thurs.-Sat.), and **Molly Malone's Irish Pub** (933 Baxter Ave., 502/473-1222, www. mollymalonesirishpub.com, 11am-2am Sun.-Wed., 11am-4am Thurs.-Sat.). Molly's draws in a large college student contingent, while O'Shea's, with its three bars and two lovely courtyards, and Flanagan's, with more than 100 beers on tap, cater to a more mixed crowd. It's not unusual to find people hopping among all three.

A newer addition to the scene, beer mecca **Holy Grale** (1034 Bardstown Rd., http:// holygralelouisville.com, 4pm-1am Mon.-Thurs., 1pm-2am Fri.-Sat.) is a temple to craft beer (and craft beer only) located in a former Unitarian church. They've got 26 taps, lots of bottles, and a good bar menu to boot, with an unbeatable indoor area and a lovely beer garden.

When the weather is nice, make **Monkey Wrench** (1025 Barret Ave., 502/582-2433,

4pm-2am Tues.-Fri., noon-2am Sat., 10am-2am Sun.) your destination. Located in a former Laundromat, this spacious bar has a fantastic rooftop deck where you can enjoy inexpensive drinks. A small cover may be charged if you opt to drink inside and enjoy the live music, but the deck is always free.

More interested in nightclubs than bars? Then **Phoenix Hill Tavern** (644 Baxter Ave., 502/589-4957, www.phoenixhill.com, 8pm-4am Wed. and Sat., 8pm-3am Thurs., 5pm-4am Fri.) is a good bet. On weekends, live music plays from three stages, and in summer, the dance party moves outdoors to the deck. Phoenix Hill also hosts national acts and special events. Check the online calendar.

Although members of the GLBQT demographic should find themselves comfortable anywhere listed here, a few Bardstown Road establishments are known for being especially gay-friendly. They aren't gay bars, but bars that are welcoming to all and have a higher percentage of GLBQT patrons than some other places. Regardless of your sexual orientation, the following sites are worth checking out for a good time. **NoWhere** (1133 Bardstown Rd., http://nowherelouisville.com, 4pm-4am Mon.-Sat., 2pm-4am Sun.) attracts a fun-loving crowd with its DJ and dance floor as well as pool tables and a chill patio. **Big Bar** (1202 Bardstown Rd., 502/618-2237, 4pm-4am Mon.-Sat., 2pm-4am Sun.), a small place despite its name, has the welcoming feel of a neighborhood bar, and its patio is great for people-watching. **Mixer** (1565 Bardstown Rd., 502/384-1565, http://mixerlouisville. com, 5pm-4am Tues.-Sun.), a piano bar with good cocktails, has a relaxed but classy atmosphere.

LIVE MUSIC
Downtown

Stevie Ray's Blues Bar (230 E. Main St., 502/387-7365, www.stevieraysbluesbar.com, 4pm-midnight Mon.-Tues., 4pm-1am Wed.-Thurs., 4pm-3am Fri., 6pm-3am Sat.) brings in some of the nation's best blues musicians as well as top local talent. Crowds regularly pack the bar, which is equally welcoming to those who like to enjoy their blues with a drink at a table and those who feel the need to get up and dance.

In the basement of the Glassworks building, **Jazzyblu** (815 W. Market St., 502/992-3243, www.jazzyblu.com, 8pm-midnight Wed., 5pm-11pm Thurs., 8pm-2am Fri.-Sat., 6pm-11pm Sun.) appeals to the artsy crowd with its upscale lounge feel and its schedule of jazz, blues, and neo soul shows.

Bardstown Road

Highlands Tap Room (1279 Bardstown Rd., 502/459-2337, www.highlandstaproom.com, 4pm-4am daily) offers live music seven days a week and never charges a cover. The music is diverse, ranging from rock and indie to blues and bluegrass, and bands are both local and regional. The bar also hosts open mic and karaoke nights. On busy nights, getting to the bar to order one of the 13 microbrews they have on tap can be difficult, but the crowd is friendly.

COMEDY CLUBS
Bardstown Road

Comedy Caravan (1250 Bardstown Rd., 502/459-0022, www.comedycaravan.com) has been making Louisville laugh for more than two decades. Nationally known comedians share the stage with up-and-coming performers, all of whom know how to tell a joke or two. Check the website for a schedule of shows. You must be 18 or older to attend. Reservations are recommended.

MOVIE THEATERS
Bardstown Road

Louisville has plenty of theaters showing blockbuster hits and offering stadium seating. But if you're looking to catch a foreign or independent film, you'll want to get a ticket at **Baxter Avenue Theatre** (1250 Bardstown Rd., 502/456-4404, www.baxter8.com). Blockbuster films are also shown. Film freaks won't want to miss Midnight at the Baxter,

a series in which cult classics appear in all their 35-mm glory on the big screen on select Saturdays.

East Louisville

For a cheap night out, screen a flick at **Village 8** (4014 Dutchmans Ln., 502/894-8697, www.village8.com), Louisville's discount theater. Tickets are only $4 in the evening, $3 before 6pm. Every Friday, a new first-run independent, foreign, or art-house film opens at Village 8 as part of the Louisville Exclusive Film series.

PERFORMING ARTS
Kentucky Center for the Performing Arts

The stages of the **Kentucky Center for the Performing Arts** (501 W. Main St., 502/562-0100, www.kentuckycenter.org) are home to the **Louisville Ballet** (www.louisvilleballet.org), **Louisville Orchestra** (www.louisvilleorchestra.org), **Kentucky Opera** (http://kentuckyopera.org), the **Broadway Across America** series (http://louisville.broadway.com), and the **Stage One** (www.stageone.org) children's theater. The center also puts on concerts, shows, and performances from nonresident groups and popular artists in a series called Kentucky Center Presents. With three stages on-site, ranging from the tiny experimental MeX to the kid-friendly Bomhard to the crowd-welcoming Whitney Hall, as well as the grand stage of the nearby Brown Theatre (315 W. Broadway), the Kentucky Center is where you go to see great performing artists from every genre. All shows draw big crowds, but for the Broadway series in particular, be sure to get tickets well in advance, as the best seats for these shows sell out quickly.

Actor's Theatre

For powerful performances of both groundbreaking and classic plays, **Actor's Theatre** (316 W. Main St., 502/584-1205, www.actorstheatre.org) is the hottest act in town. The Tony Award-winning theater is known for its daring and innovation, introducing more than 300 plays into the greater theater world and premiering three Pulitzer Prize winners. It's also known by locals for its annual production of *A Christmas Carol,* which seems to get better every year. The theater's three stages are reached through a magnificent lobby that was originally built as the imposing Bank of Louisville building in 1837.

Louisville Palace

When big-name comedians, musicians who like to provide their audience with an intimate experience, and other performers of national note come to town, you can often find them at the **Louisville Palace** (625 4th Ave., 502/583-4555, www.louisvillepalace.com). This performing arts space lives up to its high-reaching name thanks to its many visual pleasures. Built in 1928, it cost $2 million—a remarkable amount then—and you'll understand why immediately. The Spanish Baroque design translates into a lobby of bright red, gold, and blue with a vaulted ceiling featuring carvings of such greats as Shakespeare and Beethoven. Entering the theater, you'll feel as though you've stepped into a Spanish courtyard due to the plethora of arcades, balconies, and turrets, and the ceiling painted like the midnight sky. Come for the show or come for the theater; either way you'll have an amazing experience.

ART GALLERIES

Art is thriving in Louisville, with galleries popping up all around town. In fact, the gallery scene has exploded so much that two monthly hops are needed to keep patrons happy, though galleries are, of course, open outside of trolley hop hours.

◖ First Friday Trolley Hop

Since the most recent turn of the century, downtown Louisville's Main and Market Streets have transformed into the place to be for art lovers. Galleries abound, and thanks to the **First Friday Trolley Hop** (www.first-fridaytrolleyhop.com), they're all easy to visit

and welcoming to both the committed art patron and the casual browser. From 5pm-11pm on the first Friday of each month, historic trolleys circulate through the art district, offering free rides between art galleries and the nearby restaurants, bars, and shops. Galleries often hold exhibition openings on First Friday nights, while restaurants offer special menus and deals. A full listing of participating galleries with links to their individual websites can be found on the Trolley Hop website, so you can plan in advance where you want to stop. On First Fridays, most galleries stay open until 9pm. Free parking is available at Slugger Field, the Fourth Street Live! parking garage, and on the street after 6pm.

A few noteworthy galleries are **Glassworks** (815 W. Market St., 502/584-4510, www.louisvilleglassworks.com, 10am-5pm Mon.-Sat.), which has two glass studios, two glass galleries, and a workshop space where you can take classes; **Flame Run** (828 E. Market St., 502/584-5353, www.flamerun.com, 10am-4pm, Mon.-Fri., 10am-5pm Sat.), another excellent glass studio that plays host to an array of exhibitions; **Zephyr Gallery** (610 E. Market St., 502/585-5646, www.zephyrgallery.org, 11am-6pm Tues.-Sat.), a cooperative gallery with 14 members who show their work on a rotating basis; and **Pyro Gallery** (909 E. Market St., 502/587-0106, www.pyrogallery.com, noon-6pm Thurs.-Sat.), another cooperative with artists working in everything from clay to film to found objects.

F.A.T. Friday Hop

Trolley-hop fun isn't limited to the first Friday of the month; it's also scheduled for 6pm-10:30pm on the last Friday of the month, when the beloved TARC trolley makes its way to Frankfort Avenue for the **F.A.T. Friday Hop** (www.fatfridayhop.org), offering free rides to hop participants. Though the Frankfort Avenue area boasts less art galleries than downtown, it's still a bustling area of boutiques, specialty shops, and restaurants. A map of participants can be found on the F.A.T. Friday website.

Most participating galleries stay open until at least 9pm on F.A.T. Fridays.

Whether on the trolley hop or on your own time, here are a few galleries worth seeking out. The **Mellwood Art Center** (1860 Mellwood Ave., 502/895-3650, www.mellwoodartcenter.com), located in a 360,000-square-foot industrial building that once housed the Fischer Meat Packing plant, now houses more than 200 artist studios and galleries, running the entire gamut of arts and crafts. Though the center is open 9am-9pm daily, not all artists are there at all times. For the best chance of finding the artist you're looking for in studio, visit during the trolley hop or during market hours (11am-4pm Wed.-Sat.). At **Pottery Rowe** (2048 Frankfort Ave., 502/896-0877, www.potteryrowe.com, 10am-5pm Mon.-Sat.), Melvin Rowe creates outstanding pieces from clay, ranging from functional dishes to decorative ornaments. At **Kaviar Forge & Gallery** (1718 Frankfort Ave., 502/561-0377, www.craigkaviar.com, noon-6pm Wed.-Fri., noon-4pm Sat.), artist

Craig Kaviar turns out award-winning forge work and also presents pieces by other artists in his gallery.

FESTIVALS AND EVENTS
【 Kentucky Derby Festival

The Kentucky Derby might be known as the most exciting two minutes in sports, but to Louisville, the Derby lasts far longer than two minutes. In fact, thanks to the **Kentucky Derby Festival** (www.kdf.org), Derby excitement lasts for a complete two weeks.

The party kicks off on the Saturday two weeks before the Derby (which is always the first Saturday in May) with **Thunder Over Louisville,** the largest annual fireworks display in the world. For nearly 30 minutes, eight 400-foot barges anchored in the Ohio River around the Second Street Bridge shoot a barrage of pyrotechnics into the night, turning Louisville's downtown sky into an explosion of color. Crowning the show is the mile-long waterfall of fireworks that cascades down from the bridge. The celebration begins long before

© THERESA DOWELL BLACKINTON

A balloon version of Secretariat gallops down the street during the Pegasus Parade.

dark, however, with an air show that lifts off in mid-afternoon and features performances by skydive and aeronautic teams as well as flyovers by military jets. The best viewing spots are at Waterfront Park (129 E. River Rd.). Claim yours early.

Next on the agenda for most Derby Festival attendees is the **Great BalloonFest,** which takes place the weekend after Thunder, stretching from Thursday through Saturday. Events include a Balloon Glimmer at Waterfront Park on Thursday, a Rush-Hour Race departing from Bowman Field (2815 Taylorsville Rd.) at 7am on Friday, a Balloon Glow Friday night at the Kentucky Exposition Center (937 Phillips Ln.), and the Great Balloon Race departing from Bowman Field at 7am on Saturday. All balloon events are weather permitting. Also taking place on the Saturday one week before Derby is the **Derby Festival Marathon and Mini-Marathon,** both of which take runners on a tour of Louisville, including a lap around Churchill Downs.

During Derby week, the Festival really heats up, with the end of the week especially loaded with popular events. On Wednesday evening you'll want to make your way to the Waterfront for the **Great Steamboat Race** (6pm), which pits the hometown *Belle of Louisville* against the *Belle of Cincinnati.* The two boats race a course down the Ohio River and back to port, but the first boat across the finish line isn't necessarily the winner of the coveted gilded antlers. Instead, the winner is the boat that accumulates the most points in a competition involving five predesignated tasks, one being a calliope-playing contest. If you're not content to watch the race from shore, you can purchase a dinner cruise ticket for either boat.

On Thursday afternoon at 5pm, the festival's original event, the **Pegasus Parade,** gets underway. Broadway, from Campbell Street to 9th Street, is taken over by floats, marching bands, equestrian units, celebrities, clowns, and inflatables, and cheering crowds cram the sidewalks. Tickets are available for bleacher seats and chairs, but many people just bring their own blankets and lawn chairs and claim a street-side spot. If you're a true parade aficionado, get an in-depth look at the floats and performers during the Parade Preview, which takes place on the Tuesday evening before the race at the Kentucky Exposition Center.

As much as Louisville loves fireworks, balloons, and parades, by Friday of Derby week all thoughts have turned to horse racing. Though the big event is still a day away, you'll find Churchill Downs nearly as packed. Locals, who often spend Derby Day itself at parties rather than at the track, flock to Churchill Downs for the running of the **Kentucky Oaks,** a premier race for fillies established alongside the Derby in 1875. As with the Derby, the infield is open for the full day of racing, and attendance routinely tops 100,000. The scene is a bit more laid-back than on Derby Day, making it a favorite for families (Oaks Day is a school holiday in Louisville). General admission tickets, which allow you entrance to the infield and first-floor paddock, are $25 and available at the gate. Reserved seats must be purchased in conjunction with Derby tickets. After the races, one final pre-Derby event takes place: the **Barnstable Brown Party,** a Derby Eve gala attended by celebrities of every stripe. Legions of fans line up outside the home of Patricia Barnstable Brown (1700 Spring Dr.) in the hopes of spotting their favorite stars.

The denouement of all the celebrating and the reason the festival takes place at all is the **Kentucky Derby,** run every year since 1875 at Churchill Downs, making it the longest-running sporting event in the United States. Though the actual Run for the Roses is the 10th race of the day, with the traditional singing of "My Old Kentucky Home" and the call to the post taking place around 6pm, the gates at Churchill Downs open at 8am, and the racing starts at 11am. Join the more than 150,000 people who attend the Derby each year for an experience everyone should have at least once. In the grandstands, women wear extravagant hats, men wear seersucker suits, and everyone enjoys at least one mint julep. When it's time to watch the best three-year-old thoroughbreds in the nation race, all eyes turn to the track.

Overhead in Millionaires Row, Hollywood celebrities air kiss each other and pose for the camera in designer outfits. And in the 40 acres of infield, where most Derby attendees end up, anything goes. Though you can catch a glimpse of the horses passing by if you push your way up to the fence and you can see all the races on the infield's big-screen TVs, most people come to the infield to party rather than watch the horses run. The area near the third turn is particularly notorious for its raucous behavior, which almost always involves alcohol snuck in via ingenious methods and frequently involves mud, nudity, and other behavior that your parents would not approve of. But don't fear; if that's not your scene, just head toward the first turn, where families tend to congregate and even Miss Manners would find little to shake her head at. General admission tickets cost $40 and an unlimited number are available at the gate. Reserved seats are much, much harder to come by. Without a lot of money or luck, obtaining reserved seats for the Derby is nearly impossible. Tickets for the Derby and Oaks are sold together in a package. You can submit a ticket request to Churchill Downs via their website (www.churchilldowns.com), which will enter you into a lottery for tickets. Additionally, a few thousand tickets are released for public sale, again via the website, in December or January. These tickets range in price from $172 for a grandstand bleacher seat to $6,390 for a six-seat box in the third-floor clubhouse.

Aside from the Oaks and Derby, all events mentioned here are free to spectators with a Derby pin. Pins can be purchased at the entrance to all events for $5, as well as at local grocery stores, drugstores, and other retailers for $4. The Kentucky Derby Festival consists of many more events than those outlined here, so check the website for a full calendar of events with descriptions. You'll also want to confirm dates, times, and locations for all events.

Humana Festival of New American Plays

Be the first to know about the next hot thing in theater by attending the annual **Humana Festival of New American Plays** (www.actorstheatre.org). This internationally renowned festival, held for seven consecutive weeks between February and April, unveils the best new works by American playwrights. Many of these plays have gone on to win prestigious prizes. The excitement in the air is palpable. For theater buffs, attending the festival is a must. In addition to single performance tickets, packages are also available.

Forecastle Festival

Billing itself as a music/art/activism festival, the **Forecastle Festival** (http://forecastlefest.com) is a huge three-day outdoor concert. The festival, which is held at Waterfront Park in early July, features more than 100 bands and is considered one of the premier outdoor events in the nation. In 2013, performers included the Black Keys, Tift Merritt, Old Crow Medicine Show, the Avett Brothers, Big Boi, and a slew of other artists from a wide variety of genres. For many attendees, the event is as much about the experience as the music. Single-day and three-day tickets are available.

Abbey Road on the River

Though you might assume the world's largest Beatles music festival would be held in England, you'd be wrong. It's actually held in Louisville over Memorial Day weekend. At **Abbey Road on the River** (www.abbeyroadontheriver.com), more than 60 bands pay tribute to The Beatles during five days of rocking and rolling at the waterfront Belvedere Park. When the official partying ends around 1am, many attendees head to the nearby Galt House for sing-alongs of Beatles favorites. The hotel also hosts film viewings as well as a few indoor stages. If you can't get enough of John, Paul, George, and Ringo, you won't want to miss this festival. Five-day tickets offer the best value, but you can also buy single-day tickets.

Kentucky Shakespeare Festival

Every summer from mid-June to mid-July, the **Kentucky Shakespeare Festival** (www.kyshakes.org) raises the curtain on the stage

© THERESA DOWELL BLACKINTON

Saying hello to Freddy Farm Bureau is a State Fair tradition.

of late August every year, is an end-of-summer rite. From fine-arts competitions to tobacco judging, from livestock shows to beauty pageants, from the thrill of pig races to the suspense of the pipe-smoking contest, the Kentucky State Fair offers something for everyone. A huge midway, as well as a series of free and ticketed concerts, rounds out the offerings. Admire the skill of quilters, judge for yourself which goat deserves a blue ribbon, pick up as many freebies as you can carry, say hello to giant Freddy Farm Bureau, or just people watch. To fit it all in, you'll need a few days, especially if you want to take in events such as the World Championship Horse Show. You'll also want to come hungry as there's a feast of food to be had. For a real taste of the Bluegrass State, forgo the carnival classic corndog and gyro stands and instead visit the Kentucky Proud Tent for your choice of locally produced treats. The pork chop sandwiches are hard to beat. Tickets are available at the gate. Before the fair begins, discounted tickets are available at area Kroger grocery stores.

at the C. Douglas Ramsey Amphitheatre in Old Louisville's Central Park and presents two or three of the Bard's works. No matter what plays they're putting on, expect elaborate costumes, impressive scenery, and accomplished actors. Dating back to 1949, making it the oldest free and independent Shakespeare festival in the United States, Shakespeare in Central Park is a Louisville tradition and draws big crowds. The amphitheater can seat 1,000 people, but you're also welcome to view your "Free Will" from a blanket on the lawn. Bring a picnic to enjoy before the 8pm show and make it an evening.

◖ Kentucky State Fair
The **Kentucky State Fair** (Kentucky Exposition Center, 937 Phillips Ln., www.kystatefair.org), occupying an 11-day stretch

St. James Court Art Show
Fine art and fine homes go well together, which may explain why the **St. James Court Art Show** (Old Louisville, www.stjamescourtartshow.com, 10am-6pm Fri.-Sat., 10am-5pm Sun., free), which takes place in the heart of Old Louisville on the first full weekend in October, is such a well-attended event. Consistently ranked by artists and art organizations as one of the top art shows in the nation, St. James features 750 artists from across the continent. At booths set up amid the mansions on St. James and Belgravia courts as well as on Magnolia, 3rd, and 4th Streets, you'll find works in 16 mediums, ranging from fiber to clay, metal, wood, and photography—and in price ranges to fit any budget. Artists are chosen through a competitive selection process, and all work is juried.

Shopping

SHOPPING DISTRICTS

Like every midsize city in the United States, Louisville has its share of shopping malls and big box stores, but it also has some great local stores. Shopaholics will want to hit NuLu, Frankfort Avenue, and Bardstown Road to find the best Louisville goods.

NuLu

Currently the hottest area in town, NuLu stretches from Main Street on the north to Jefferson Street on the south, and from Hancock Street on the west to Wenzel Street on the east, with most of the action clustered on Market Street in the middle. It's all easily walkable, so take an afternoon to stroll from shop to shop, stopping for drinks and food when the urge hits. Can't-miss stops include **Gifthorse** (805 E. Market St., 502/681-5576, 11am-6pm Tues.-Thurs., 11am-7pm Fri.-Sat.), an awesome

© THERESA DOWELL BLACKINTON

sweets for sale at Muth's Candies

source for fun fashion and gifts, much of them locally made; **Revolver** (707 E. Market St., 502/468-6130, www.revolverlouisville.com, 10am-5pm Tues.-Thurs. and Sat., 10am-6pm Fri., 11am-3pm Sun.), with drool-worthy furnishings and home decor; **Joe Ley Antiques** (615 E. Market St., 502/583-4014, www.joeley. com, 10am-5pm Tues.-Sat.), which overwhelms with two acres of amazing antiques; **Muth's Candies** (630 E. Market St., 502/585-2952, www.muthscandy.com, 8:30am-4pm Tues.-Fri., 10am-4pm Sat.), Louisville's confectionary since 1921; **Taste Fine Wines and Bourbons** (634 E. Market St., 502/409-4646, http://taste-finewinesandbourbons.com, 11am-8pm Tues.-Wed., noon-late Thurs.-Fri., 10:30am-late Sat.), where you can sample and buy a wide variety of the namesake products; and the **Louisville Beer Store** (746 E. Market St., 502/569-2337, www.louisvillebeerstore.com, 3pm-10pm Tues.-Thurs., 1pm-midnight Fri., noon-midnight Sat., 1pm-7pm Sun.), which has hundreds of craft beers by the bottle as well as eight rotating taps and a tasting bar.

Frankfort Avenue

Frankfort Avenue, with a long history as a central area for local business, is another good place to pound the pavement in search of fun finds. If you're after high fashion, pop in at **Peacock Boutique** (2828 Frankfort Ave., 502/897-1158, www.shopthepeacock.com, 10am-7pm Mon.-Sat.), or for a more budget-friendly option, try **Margaret's Consignment** (2700 Frankfort Ave., 502/896-4706, www. margaretsconsignment.com, 10am-5pm Mon.-Sat., noon-4pm Sun.), which specializes in higher-end clothing. If you're looking to outfit your home, browse the 20th-century antiques at **2023** (2023 Frankfort Ave., 502/899-9872, 11am-5pm Tues.-Sat.) or the fair-trade goods from 35 developing nations at **Just Creations** (2722 Frankfort Ave., 502/897-7319, www.just-creations.org, 10am-6pm Mon.-Sat.).

Bardstown Road

The Highlands is a true Louisville original, a neighborhood chock full of well-loved houses and local shops, bars, and restaurants, and Bardstown Road is the epicenter of it all. For shoppers, the one-mile stretch between Eastern Parkway and Baxter Avenue is full of fun and funky options. If you're looking for an original Louisville souvenir, such as a T-shirt that you won't find anywhere else, drop in at **WHY Louisville** (1583 Bardstown Rd., 502/456-5400, www.whylouisville.com, 11am-8pm Mon.-Fri., 10am-8pm Sat., noon-6pm Sun.), where all the goods are made by local and regional designers. You can also find cool T-shirts at nearby **Dot Fox** (1567 Bardstown Rd., 502/452-9191, www.dotfoxclothingculture.com, 11am-8pm Mon.-Thurs., 11am-9pm Fri.-Sat., noon-6pm Sun.), a local take on Urban Outfitters where trendy clothing is sold alongside kitsch. For more fashion fun, head down the street to **General Eccentric** (1600 Bardstown Rd., 502/458-8111, www.geneccentric.com, 11am-8pm Mon.-Thurs., 11am-9pm Fri.-Sat., noon-6pm Sun.), where you can always find the latest trends, though if you like it, you'd better buy it, since they stock limited quantities of each style. You'll also want to be sure to visit **Carmichael's** (1295 Bardstown Rd., 502/456-6950, www.carmichaelsbookstore.com, 8am-10pm Sun.-Thurs., 8am-11pm Fri.-Sat.), Louisville's favorite bookstore, winning over customers with its book-loving sales staff, its handpicked collection, and its neighborhood feel.

ARTS AND CRAFTS

Since 1815, **Louisville Stoneware** (731 Brent St., 502/582-1900, www.louisvillestoneware.com, 10am-6pm Mon.-Fri., 10am-5pm Sat.) has been providing the Derby City with original dinnerware and house decor. The stoneware—designed, fired, and painted at the Brent Street studio—comes in a variety of motifs and colors, both traditional and modern. The mint julep cups, Hot Brown trays, and Kentucky Pie plates make great souvenirs, and the Equine and Fleur de Lis patterns are very popular. If you'd like to see the stoneware being created, visit at 10:30am or 1:30pm, when studio tours are offered for $7. If none of the designs suit your fancy, then you're welcome to paint your own stoneware. The $25 paint-your-own price includes a tour.

Though it has a shorter history than Louisville Stoneware—dating back to 1940—**Hadley Pottery** (1570 Story Ave., 502/584-2171, www.hadleypottery.com, 9am-5pm Mon.-Fri., 9am-3pm Sat.) is also a well-loved local institution. The "Hadley blue" paint appearing on all the pottery is instantly recognizable, and the whimsical designs, originally created by Mary Alice Hadley and now painted by her protégées, have a strong fan base. The holiday plates make for fun collector's items, and kids in particular love the animal designs. Many of the items can be personalized. Hadley Pottery is sold throughout the country, but the factory in Louisville is where it's all created, and you're welcome to take a tour (2pm Mon.-Thurs.) as well as browse the showroom.

MALLS

Louisville's most popular indoor malls are located directly next to each other. **Mall St. Matthews** (5000 Shelbyville Rd., 502/893-0311, www.mallstmatthews.com) is anchored by Dillards and J. C. Penney, while **Oxmoor Center** (7900 Shelbyville Rd., 502/426-3000, www.oxmoorcenter.com) is anchored by Sears, Macy's, and Von Maur. **The Paddock Shops** (4300 Summit Plaza Dr., 502/425-3441), an outdoor shopping center with such popular stores as Banana Republic, J.Crew, and Pier 1, is another favored shopping destination.

Sports and Recreation

PARKS

More than a hundred parks dot Louisville, providing 14,000 acres of green space, so no matter where you are, there's a park nearby. To find the one that most suits your interests, visit the Metro Parks website (http://louisvilleky.gov/metroparks) and use the Park Finder, which allows you to search by name, location, or park amenities.

◖ Olmsted Park System

Although landscape architect Frederick Law Olmsted is probably best known for New York's Central Park, many critics consider the park system he designed for Louisville to be his greatest accomplishment. Locals certainly think so. Consisting of three large flagship parks—Cherokee, Iroquois, and Shawnee—connected by six tree-lined parkways, with 15 smaller parks and playgrounds along the way, Louisville's **Olmsted Park System** (www.olmstedparks.org) is where Louisvillians go for a breath of fresh air.

CHEROKEE PARK

Cherokee Park (Willow Ave. and Cherokee Pkwy.) is the most popular park in the city, drawing nearly 500,000 visitors annually. In the Beargrass Creek Valley, Cherokee's 409 acres boast wide-open spaces perfect for picnics and pick-up games and broad vistas that reward hikers, joggers, and bikers. The always-busy 2.4-mile Scenic Loop is a mixed-use, one-way road, with one lane for cars and another dedicated to person-powered transport. Other favorite areas include the sport-lover's Frisbee Field, the dog run at Cochran Hill, the playground at Hogan's Fountain, and the eternal hangout of Big Rock. The park also sports an archery range, bird sanctuary, nine-hole golf course, and a series of trails shared by hikers and mountain bikers. Thanks to Cherokee Park's many entrances and exits, even locals are known to get confused when driving through,

so it's best to consult the park and trail maps online to plan your outing.

IROQUOIS PARK

The southern anchor of the Olmsted Park System, **Iroquois Park** (Southern Pkwy. and Taylor Blvd.) is known for its rugged terrain and the 10,000-plus-year-old forest that constitutes the heart of the park. From the park summit, home to one of many outlooks that dot Iroquois's 739 acres, visitors can take in a grand panorama of Louisville. Take a bike up to the summit for a challenge, or test your athletic prowess on the basketball courts, disc golf course, or 18-hole golf course. The Iroquois amphitheater, home to warm-weather productions and concerts, is another highlight of the park.

SHAWNEE PARK

Shawnee Park (Southwestern Pkwy. and Broadway), in western Louisville, makes the most of its riverfront setting with a Great Lawn popular for family reunions and other large gatherings. The basketball courts, baseball fields, and tennis courts are often busy, and the 18-hole golf course is the only city park course to offer a complete driving range facility.

Waterfront Park

Encompassing 85 acres of riverfront real estate in downtown Louisville, **Waterfront Park** (www.louisvillewaterfront.com, 6am-11pm daily) is home to most of the city's outdoor celebrations. Huge crowds gather on the Great Lawn and its surrounding green spaces for **Thunder Over Louisville,** the kickoff to the Derby Festival, as well as the **Waterfront Independence Festival,** a celebration of music and fireworks every July 3 and 4. The park also hosts numerous smaller festivals, concerts, and fundraiser walk/runs. In the summer, outdoor yoga classes and **Waterfront Wednesday,** a free after-work concert series scheduled for

© THERESA DOWELL BLACKINTON

taking a walk on the Big 4 Pedestrian & Bicycle Bridge at Waterfront Park

the last Wednesday of each month, are popular with downtown workers and visitors. Visit the park's website for a complete listing of the many events held here each year.

It doesn't take a festival, however, for the park to be bustling. It's a prime spot for a picnic, a bike ride, a walk, or a pick-up game of ultimate Frisbee or touch football. For kids, the playground and waterplay areas are the biggest draws. For a place to sit quietly and thick, try the Lincoln Memorial, which celebrates Abe's connections to the state. The most recent addition, the **Big 4 Pedestrian & Bicycle Bridge,** is a big hit. This converted railroad bridge over the Ohio River connects Louisville with Jeffersonville, Indiana, and is a great place to get some exercise with a view. Parking is available on the street and in lots, most of which are free, along River Road.

Passing through Waterfront Park is the **Louisville Loop** (www.louisvilleloop.org), an approximately 100-mile multiuse trail that, when completed, will encircle the city. It is

divided into five sections, three of which are completely or partially completed and open to the public, and two of which were still in the planning phases at the time of research. The biggest complete section is the 23-mile stretch of the Ohio River Valley section, running from Waterfront Park to Farnsley-Moremen Landing. Other open sections of the trail include 1.5 miles of the Shale Lowland section in southwest central Jefferson County and two miles of the Floyds Fork section in the far eastern section of the county. Visit the website for updated information and trail access points.

Louisville Extreme Park

The **Louisville Extreme Park** (Clay St. and Franklin St., www.louisvilleextremepark.org, 6am-11pm daily) features a 24-foot pipe, seven bowls ranging 4-11 feet, a 12-foot wooden vertical ramp, and plenty of ledges and rails, which invite skateboarders, in-line skaters, and bikers to show off their best moves. A rating system similar to that used on ski slopes identifies areas suitable for those with beginner, intermediate, and advanced skills. Don't forget your helmet; a local ordinance requires a helmet to be worn by all park users.

E. P. "Tom" Sawyer State Park

The only state park in Louisville, **E. P. "Tom" Sawyer State Park** (3000 Freys Hill Rd., 502/429-3280, http://parks.ky.gov, daylight-dark, free) doesn't lack for anything. Among its more standard offerings are a basketball and badminton gym, 12 tennis courts, a plethora of fields (14 soccer, 5 lacrosse, 3 softball, 1 rugby), fitness and nature trails, and picnic shelters. A number of leagues use these facilities, and information about joining one can be found on the park's website. The park's less common features include a model airplane airfield, an archery range, and a BMX track (Mar.-Oct.). A four-acre dog park welcomes canines and their companions, and an Olympic-size pool (noon-6pm Sun.-Fri., 11am-6pm Sat., Memorial Day weekend-Labor Day, $5 ages 13 and up, $4 ages 3-12) is a park favorite. For a unique treat, take part in one of the monthly Star Parties

© THERESA DOWELL BLACKINTON

water-spraying fish at Waterfront Park

sponsored by the Louisville Astronomical Society and held at the park (www.louisville-astro.org).

The Parklands of Floyds Fork

One of the city's most exciting outdoor projects since the creation of the Olmsted Park System, the **Parklands of Floyds Fork** (http://theparklands.org) is an in-progress work in Eastern Louisville, which, when finished in 2015, will consist of four parks connected by a park drive, about a hundred miles of hike and bike trails, and 19 miles of canoe trails. At the time of research, Beckley Creek Park was open, Pope Lick Park was set to open, and ground was being broken on Turkey Run Park and Broad Run Park. Visit the website for updated information.

HIKING

Covering a remarkable 6,218 acres, **Jefferson Memorial Forest** (11311 Mitchell Hill Rd., 502/368-5404, www.memorialforest.com, 8am-dusk daily) is the largest municipal urban forest in the United States. Hikers in particular love this park, as it offers more than 35 miles of trails. The longest and most challenging of these is the 6.2-mile, one-way Siltstone Trail, while the 0.2-mile Tuliptree Trail is the shortest and easiest (it's also wheelchair accessible). In between these two are a multitude of one-way and loop trails offering hikes of varying degrees of difficulty. Whichever you choose, you'll get to enjoy the bountiful plant life—50 types of trees and 17 species of ferns—as well as wildlife not often found in an urban setting—bobcats, coyotes, red foxes, white-tailed deer, great blue herons, and horned owls. For bird-watchers, a bird blind is available by appointment.

GOLF
Louisville Metro Parks

Nine of Louisville's Metro Parks feature public golf courses (http://louisvilleky.gov/metroparks/golf), with six of these offering a full 18 holes. Varying in difficulty, the courses invite golfers of all abilities to play at affordable prices. Of the nine courses, the two most popular are **Seneca Golf Course** (2300 Pee Wee Reese Rd., 502/458-9298) and **Charlie Vettiner Golf Course** (10207 Mary Dell Ln., 502/267-9958). Seneca, with its hilly par-72 course running aside Beargrass Creek, has been ranked the sixth most difficult course in the state, while Charlie Vettiner, with 50 sand traps and three ponds, is ranked right behind Seneca as the seventh most challenging.

Quail Chase

Boasting country club standards without the membership fees, **Quail Chase** (7000 Cooper Chapel Rd., 502/239-2110, www.quailchase.com) is a public golf course with 27 championship regulation holes. Water hazards, bunkers, and tree-lined fairways make every round a challenge.

Valhalla

The premier golf course in Louisville, **Valhalla** (15503 Shelbyville Rd., 502/245-4475, http://valhalla.pgalinks.com) is a private club that has hosted the PGA Championship, the

Senior PGA Championship, and the Ryder Cup. Valhalla is partially owned by the PGA and considered a difficult course by even the world's best golfers. If you're a top-notch golfer and want to give the course a go yourself, you'll need to be the guest of a member or arrange guest privileges through the club. Check the website for details of upcoming events if you'd like to be a spectator.

SWIMMING

The **Mary T. Meagher Aquatic Center** (201 Reservoir Ave., 502/897-9949, http://louisvilleky.gov/metroparks), named for Louisville's own Olympic champion, features an indoor Olympic-size pool open year-round for both exercise and recreational swimming. The pool is open 5am-9pm Monday-Friday and 9am-6pm on Saturdays, but recreational swim is restricted to noon-3:30pm Monday-Friday with the addition of a 7pm-9pm time slot on Friday, and noon-6pm on Saturday. Swim lessons, exercise classes, and lifeguarding classes are offered at the center. A day pass costs $4.50 for those over age 13, while those 12 and under pay $2.25. For frequent users, a membership is the best option.

BIKING

Bike Louisville is an effort of the city government to encourage biking. To map a route, find roads with bike lanes, connect to local bike organizations, or find a bike shop, visit http://louisvilleky.gov/bikelouisville. Among the most popular places for road biking in the city are Cherokee and Iroquois parks and Jefferson Memorial Forest. Mountain bikers also like Cherokee and Iroquois, while BMX bikers stake claim to E. P. "Tom" Sawyer State Park.

Bike Clubs

The **Louisville Bicycle Club** (www.louisvillebicycleclub.org) organizes rides and events and advocates for cyclists. If you're looking for a group to ride with, check the calendar on their website, as they have rides scheduled nearly every day. The LBC also sponsors the annual **Old Kentucky Home Tour,** a two-day ride with

route options of 50, 72, and 102 miles. The century route takes riders from E. P. "Tom" Sawyer State Park to Bardstown, Kentucky, where they overnight before returning the next day.

Bike Shops and Rentals

For all your biking needs, visit **Bardstown Road Bicycle Co.** (1051 Bardstown Rd., 502/485-9795, www.bardstownroadbicycles.com, 10am-7pm Mon.-Wed., 10am-5pm Thurs.-Sat.), where the knowledgeable staff can help you pick out a new bike, fix up an old bike, or gear up for any type of bike adventure. They also rent bikes.

At **Wheel Fun Rentals** (Waterfront Park at the Big 4 Bridge, 502/589-2453, www.wheelfunrentals.com, 10am-9pm mid-May-mid-Aug., hours are weather-dependent rest of the year), you can rent a bicycle and explore Louisville's downtown and waterfront. Bikes available for rental range from your standard cruiser to tandem bikes to a double surrey that can transport your entire family.

SPECTATOR SPORTS
Horse Racing

Under the iconic spires of **Churchill Downs** (700 Central Ave., 502/636-4400, www.churchilldowns.com, $3 general admission), the world-famous Kentucky Derby is run every year on the first Saturday of May. The racetrack also hosts a spring meet (late April-early July), a Homecoming meet (September), and a fall meet (late October-November), where you can experience a full day of thoroughbred racing on both dirt and turf at the historic track. Pick up a program, wander over to the paddock for an up-close look at the contenders and their jockeys, place a bet, and then hurry down to the rail to cheer your pick on to the finish line. It's a classic way to pass a day in the Derby City. For a twist on traditional horse racing, check out Downs After Dark, a Saturday night racing event that tends to draw a younger crowd.

College Sports

Consistently drawing some of the largest crowds

WIN, PLACE, OR SHOW: PLACING A BET AT CHURCHILL DOWNS

First, get a program. You're going to need to know what horses are racing, and you might want to know what jockey is on board what horse, what the horses' previous race results are, or maybe just what color silks the jockeys will be wearing. There are as many ways of picking a winner as there are people, ranging from complicated mathematical formulas to lucky numbers and colors, so go with whatever feels right to you.

Second, scan the tote board to see the current odds for each horse. They change continually as people place bets. At Churchill Downs, odds are listed as a single number, such as 5. This translates to 5 to 1 odds, which means that you'd get a $5 payout for every $1 bet if said horse wins. Though there are payouts for second and third places, the winnings are impossible to calculate until the race has been run because they vary based on which three horses end up in the money and in what order. It's complicated. Don't worry about it.

Third, once you've picked a horse, decide how much you want to bet (there's a $2 minimum), and whether you want to bet on the horse to win, place (finish second), or show (finish third). Be aware that if you bet a horse to place, you get a payout if it wins or places, and if you bet a horse to show, you get a pay-out if it wins, places, or shows. The payout for a show bet on a winning horse isn't as much as the payout on a win bet, however.

Fourth, once you're certain you've picked the winner, head to the betting window. Approach the teller and place the bet. To make sure the teller gets all the info straight, give him or her your bet in the following manner: "Xth race, X dollars to (win, place, show) on horse number X." (For example: "Fourth race, two dollars to win on number four.") Check your ticket before walking away from the window to make sure all the information is correct.

Finally, return to your seat and scream your lungs out in an effort to get your horse to cross the finish line first. If your horse does win (or place or show, depending on your wager), wait until the results are posted as final and then return to the betting window, where the teller will cash your ticket.

Once you've gotten the hang of the straight bet, you can venture into the world of exactas (pick in correct order the first- and second-place finishers), trifectas (pick in correct order the first-, second-, and third-place finishers), pick threes (pick the winner of three designated races), and other exotic wagers, which someone at the race track will gladly explain to you if you just ask nicely. Good luck!

winning Kentucky Derby ticket

MORE THAN A RIVALRY: THE NATION'S BIGGEST HIGH SCHOOL FOOTBALL GAME

On a Friday evening in late September, more than 35,000 fans pack Papa John's Cardinal Stadium to watch a football game, but not one played by the University of Louisville. Instead, these fans, wearing St. Xavier green-and-gold or Trinity green-and-white sweatshirts, face paint, and hats, have come to watch Louisville's two largest Catholic all-male high schools have it out on the gridiron. It's the nation's best high school football rivalry.

Year in and year out, one, if not both, of these teams end up in the state championship game, but to many players and fans, the annual **St. X-Trinity game** is just as important,

if not more so. Sure, the approximately 1,400 students from each high school attend, but so also do their parents, neighbors, friends, and their friends' friends. Alumni turn out with their families in tow, some coming all the way across the country to what has become an unofficial annual reunion. Tailgating reaches a fever pitch in the parking lot pregame, though officials do ask that you keep it alcohol-free. Going far beyond a high school event, the St. X-Trinity game is a Louisville event, so no matter what your connection is, you'll want to join the crazed fans in seeing high school football like you've never seen it before.

---

in college athletics, the **University of Louisville Cardinals** (502/852-5732, www.uoflsports.com), who will join the ACC in 2014 after years in the Big East, are Louisville's team. The men's basketball team, NCAA 2013 National Champions, are the crowd favorite, packing in the fans at every one of their home games at the 22,000-seat **KFC Yum! Center** (S. 2nd St. and W. Main St). The basketball rivalry with the cross-state Kentucky Wildcats is rabid, and was made even more so when the University of Louisville landed Rick Pitino as their head coach in 2001. For many Wildcat fans, this made Pitino a bigger traitor than Benedict Arnold himself, as Pitino had led the Cats for eight years in the 1990s, but for Louisville fans it was the coup of the century. No matter whom they're playing, however, expect exciting hoops and fans who live and die Cards basketball.

Behind men's basketball, U of L football is the passion of local fans, who religiously fill the 56,000 seats of **Papa John's Cardinal Stadium** (2800 S. Floyd St.) and go whole-hog in pregame tailgating. A stretch of highly successful seasons was crowned by a victory over Florida at the 2013 Sugar Bowl.

Though overshadowed by men's basketball, the women's basketball program is also

top-notch, playing for the national championship most recently in 2013, which was one of the best years ever for the Cardinals in general. The women share KFC Yum! Center with the men's team.

Additionally, the Louisville baseball team has come into its own in the past decade, making their second appearance in the College World Series in 2013. The team plays at Jim Patterson Stadium (Central Ave. and 3rd St.).

Tickets for men's basketball games are nearly impossible to come by, so your best bet is to check www.stubhub.com to find someone selling theirs. For other sports, tickets may be purchased online at www.ticketmaster.com or at the **U of L Ticket Offices** (Belknap Campus, Student Activities Center, 3rd floor, corner of Floyd St. and Brandeis St., 502/852-5863, or Papa John's Cardinal Stadium Gate 2, 9am-5pm Mon.-Fri. and starting at 9am game days).

Professional Baseball

As the AAA affiliate of the Cincinnati Reds, the **Louisville Bats** (502/212-2287, www.milb.com) offer baseball fans a chance to see tomorrow's big-league stars in an intimate setting. The Bats play home games at **Louisville Slugger Field** (401 E. Main St.), a 13,000-seat stadium with views of downtown and the Ohio River. The stadium, which opened in 2000, preserves a part of historic Louisville in that it incorporates the Brinly-Hardy Warehouse, a train shed built in 1889, into its design. With tickets starting at $7, a Bats game at Slugger Field makes for a fun date, a night out with friends, or a family outing. Come early to get autographs, then enjoy the game, knowing that if the kids get restless, there are two in-stadium playgrounds, a carousel, a speed pitch activity, and the never-ending antics of mascot Buddy Bat.

Accommodations

Most visitors to Louisville will want to reserve a room in one of the downtown hotels or Old Louisville B&Bs. From either of these two areas, you can easily access the city's major sights and restaurants. If you don't mind being a little bit out of the action, East Louisville has two nice options as well. Look for weekend deals downtown when business travelers have gone home, and midweek specials at the B&Bs. Prices soar all over town at Derby time, and you'll also find higher prices in Old Louisville during the St. James Court Art Show.

DOWNTOWN
$100-150
One of Louisville's golden-era hotels, the four-star **Brown Hotel** (335 W. Broadway, 502/583-1234, www.brownhotel.com, $107-499) offers all the luxuries one expects from a hotel built in the high-rolling 1920s: a grand lobby fit for movie star entrances, marble flooring, mahogany furniture, and faultless service. If you can afford it, spring for one of the spacious suites, which honor the formal English Renaissance architecture of the hotel while remaining entirely comfortable. The deluxe rooms can be small, but worth the price if ambience is your interest. Located in the theater district, the Brown is within easy walking distance of all downtown attractions.

$150-200
Although the current **Galt House** (140 N. 4th St., 502/589-5200, www.galthouse.com, $145-350) dates back to only 1971, the establishment's first incarnation played host to the likes of Jefferson Davis and Charles Dickens in the 1800s. Now the Galt House is the largest hotel in Kentucky and the only waterfront hotel in Louisville, its twin towers a distinctive part of the downtown skyline. For a view out onto the Ohio River, choose one of the 591 rooms in the Rivue Tower. Deluxe rooms are spacious but not special, while suites have the luxury of balconies, wet bars, and an extra half-bath. For an upgrade, choose the neighboring Suite Tower, which offers 600 premium rooms decked out with all the amenities. The hotel is often used for large conventions, so you may want to inquire whom you will be sharing the hotel with when you reserve a room.

If you're a *Great Gatsby* fan, then you can't pass on a night at the downtown **Seelbach Hotel** (500 4th St., 502/585-3200, www.seelbachhilton.com, $169-209), the inspiration for the site of Tom and Daisy Buchanan's wedding. Though now part of the Hilton family, the Seelbach still clings to the old-world elegance that has attracted the likes of F. Scott Fitzgerald, Al Capone, and John F. Kennedy. Rooms have a somewhat standard Hilton feel with some era-appropriate touches. Get out of your room to have a bourbon in the Oak Room alcove where Capone played cards, sneak a peek at the Grand Ballroom that inspired Fitzgerald, and admire the medieval style of the Rathskellar, the only surviving Rookwood Pottery room in the world.

Over $200
If you like modern, artsy, hip hotels, then check yourself into 🄲 **21C Museum Hotel** (700 W. Main St., 502/217-6300, www.21chotel.com, $229-439), the most innovative hotel in the

FINDING ACCOMMODATIONS FOR THE DERBY

Locating a place to rest your bones during Derby week, especially on Derby weekend, is not easy. It's also not cheap. But with persistence, a willingness to compromise, and a bit of money saved up, you can find something to fit your taste and budget.

If you're committed to doing the Derby in high style, then you'll want to stay at one of downtown Louisville's classic hotels. In order to make this a reality, you must do two things: 1) plan early, and 2) pay the big bucks. It's not uncommon for Derby regulars to book their room for next year when they arrive for the current year's Derby. For a choice of rooms, you'll want to begin planning by January, though you can pick through leftovers into early spring. Most of the downtown hotels only offer rooms as part of package deals and usually have a two- or three-night minimum. Expect to pay thousands of dollars for a weekend stay.

The B&Bs of Old Louisville also offer an excellent Derby experience, particularly if you like intimate spaces and the opportunity to get really personalized advice on how to best enjoy the Derby. They are also very well located, just 2.5 miles from Churchill Downs. Unfortunately, the biggest of Louisville's B&Bs have no more than eight rooms, and some have as few as two. This means that they book up quickly, often with repeat customers. Expect to pay rates much higher than average if you do manage to find a room.

For those less picky about the ambience of their accommodations, but desirous of a location within city limits, Louisville's chain hotels offer the best option. Come Derby Day you'll find that almost all of them are at capacity, but they don't fill as quickly as the local hotels, giving you a little more time to get your plans together. Be aware that you won't find any deals here, however. Prices generally start around $300 for a typical double room. Visit a hotel aggregator website such as www.hotels.com to sort through your options.

If $300 for the Holiday Inn sounds ludicrous to you, then start looking farther afield. Once you get outside of Louisville and the immediate surrounding communities, you'll find prices that more closely resemble regular rates. You'll have to drive further and won't have all the amenities of the city, but if your main goal is to make it to the Derby without breaking the bank, this is the way to go. Begin by checking for hotels in Southern Indiana (New Albany, Jeffersonville, Clarksville), La Grange, and Shepherdsville, where prices will range greatly but be more affordable overall. You can also consider making the Derby just part of a Kentucky vacation, opening up hotel possibilities in Bardstown (30 miles), Frankfort (50 miles), and Lexington (70 miles).

Finally, go local and look for apartments, condos, and homes available for lease during Derby week. More than a few Louisvillians move in with friends and family for the weekend, renting their digs to out-of-towners. For large groups, this can be an especially good deal. Check the vacation rental and sublet sections of www.craigslist.org for available properties, as well as www.vrbo.com.

state and recipient of endless honorifics. Every one of the 90 rooms in this boutique hotel incorporates contemporary art into its design, but in no way is 21C too cool for school. Southern hospitality is the rule here, and the hotel doesn't just cover all the bases—it goes above and beyond with amenities like iPods, flat-screen HDTVs, wireless Internet, and silver mint julep cups in each room. Look for the red penguins adorning the roof of this hotel right in the heart of Museum Row.

OLD LOUISVILLE
$50-100

The three rooms at **Gallery House** (1386 S. 6th St., 502/922-6329, www.thegalleryhouse.com, $85-95) offer the most affordable stay in Old Louisville, though you should be aware that despite the home's High Victorian appearance, it was actually built in 1997 after a fire destroyed the previous property. The spirit of the house remains true to the neighborhood, and you'll enjoy the fact that all rooms have en suite bathrooms and modern systems. Plus it's hard to find owners better suited to the job: Gordon is an artist, meaning you'll find original artwork all over the house, and Leah is a chef, known for making some of the best cakes in town, so you can bet that breakfast will be a treat.

$100-150

Slip back in time at **1888 Historic Rocking Horse Manor Bed and Breakfast** (1022 S. 3rd St., 502/583-0408, www.rockinghorse-bb.com, $105-195), a meticulously restored Richardsonian Romanesque mansion in the heart of Old Louisville. The attention to architectural detail—original stained glass, relaxing claw-foot soaking tubs, and splendidly carved fireplace mantels—is matched only by the attention afforded each guest by the innkeepers, who serve a delicious two-course breakfast each morning and provide snacks and drinks in the evening. Each of the six rooms is tastefully decorated in period style and has its own bathroom. For a splurge, go for the Victorian Suite with its king-size canopy bed and hot tub.

Although the six rooms—all of which are named for the innkeeper's family members—at **Aleksander House Bed and Breakfast** (1213 S. 1st St., 502/637-4985, www.aleksanderhouse.com, $115-209) have distinct feels, the overall vibe of this 1882 Victorian mansion is warm and inviting, like the French Impressionist paintings in the dining room. Among Aleksander House's more unique offerings is a suite that can sleep 4-6 people, making it perfect for a family or girlfriend getaway. Additionally, the gourmet breakfast menu offers equally delicious options for vegans, diabetics, and celiacs.

Austin's Inn Place (915 S. 1st St., 502/585-8855, www.austinsinnplace.com, $135-155) combines two three-story houses to offer guests a choice of eight rooms, each fitted with either a king or queen bed with top-of-the-line bedding. The expansive inn also offers plenty of communal space, including a library, bar, game room, and garden. Exposed red brick

features throughout the inn, which was once the home of Kentucky governor Augustus Everett Willson. For those who rise before it's time for the full breakfast, a spread of tea, coffee, juice, cereal, fruit, and pastries will help tide you over.

Thanks to its great columned portico and Greek Revival style, the **Columbine Bed and Breakfast** (1707 S. 3rd St., 502/635-5000, www.thecolumbine.com, $125-175) stands out in this neighborhood of Victorian homes. Guests also love its sunny porches, welcoming back garden, friendly innkeepers, and breakfasts with a raved-about homemade syrup. Built for a mahogany magnate in 1896, the house is filled with this sumptuous wood. It's also remarkably well decorated, with the six large rooms classic and understated. If you fear frilliness, lace, and floral decor, then this is the B&B for you. The only negative is that bathrooms, though private, are often across the hall, but the plush bathrobes provided make this only a minor inconvenience.

One of the most magnificent homes on what was once known as Millionaires' Row, the 20,000-square-foot **Culbertson Mansion** (1432 S. 3rd St., 502/634-3100, www.culbertsonmansion.us, $109-179) boasts more than 50 rooms, all decadently decorated, including the seven bedrooms available to guests. Built by Samuel Culbertson, president of Churchill Downs during the 1920s and 1930s and the man behind the garland of roses awarded to the Derby winner, the mansion was home to many formal dinner parties and dances. Now whether you're entering through the marble mosaic door, savoring breakfast at the original dining table, having a complimentary drink with the hosts in the downstairs bar, or relaxing amid the 100 varieties of roses in the formal courtyard, you'll feel like an honored guest. Splurge for the Knights of Kentucky Suite, replete with its own baby grand piano, and you'll feel like royalty.

$150-200

Built for the wealthy industrialist family for which it is named, the **DuPont Mansion**

(1317 S. 4th St., 502/638-0045, www.dupontmansion.com, $129-239) is a conscientiously restored 1879 Italianate mansion with details that will make your jaw drop. While you eat breakfast under sparkling chandeliers, enjoy the murals covering the wall of the dining room. In the evening, take your snack of homemade goodies and wine in the formal gardens. And at night, luxuriate in the whirlpool tub found in each of the B&B's seven rooms. All of the rooms are elegant and decorated with period furniture and reproductions, but the two suites are particularly magnificent. If the DuPont Mansion is all booked up, check the availability at **Inn at the Park** (1332 S. 4th St., 502/638-0045, www.innatpark.com, $129-209), a sister property just across the street with eight rooms with private baths.

Step through the triple entry of the Richardsonian Romanesque **Bernheim Mansion** (1416 S. 3rd St., 502/638-1387, www.bernheimmansion.com, $119-225), and you'll immediately notice the abundance of exotic woods and intricate woodwork, as well as the curved stairwell lit by stained glass windows. This B&B is heavy on style and true to its roots as the home of distiller and philanthropist Bernhard Bernheim. If you're looking for luxury, choose between the Bernheim Suite and the Carriage House. The Bernheim Suite swells with old-world charm and includes a private library and office. The Carriage House impresses with its soaring 30-foot wood ceiling and exposed beams, combining contemporary architecture with antique decor. Of the remaining three rooms, one has a king bed with antique bath (but no shower), and the other two are queen rooms with a shared bath.

True to its 1884 origins but with the modern amenities travelers love, **Central Park Bed and Breakfast** (1353 S. 4th St., 502/638-1505, www.centralparkbandb.com, $135-195) offers three guest rooms on the second floor, three on the third floor, and a carriage house out back. Each room has a queen or king bed and its own private bathroom. The Rose Garden Room is especially spacious at 700 square feet, with its own sitting room with a bird's-eye view of the area. A large breakfast is served in the dining room, and other common spaces inside and out are open to guests.

EAST LOUISVILLE
$100-150

Once you enter the **Inn at Woodhaven** (401 S. Hubbards Ln., 888/895-1011, www.innatwoodhaven.com, $119-255), a 19th-century Gothic Revival home painted a cheery yellow, you'll forget that the inn is located next to an apartment complex. Beautifully decorated with period furniture, the inn makes sure no detail is forgotten. Choose among four rooms in the main house, three rooms in the carriage house out back, or the octagonal Rose Cottage. The main house's Attic Room is bigger than most apartments; in fact, the bathroom, with its spa tub and steam shower for two, is bigger than most hotel rooms. Enjoy the three-course gourmet breakfast in the dining room or in the comfort of your own room.

While most Louisville B&Bs are from the Victorian era, **Tucker House Bed and Breakfast** (2406 Tucker Station Rd., 502/297-8007, www.tuckerhouse1840.com, $105-125) transports you to the era of antebellum country living, with its four bed chambers, dining areas, and living areas all decorated true to the 1840s. Located a bit outside of town, the brick Federal-style Tucker House is a great place to stay if you're looking for a true getaway, especially if you love peace and quiet and the great outdoors. Bring your hiking shoes to explore the five acres of woods and the spring-fed lake. As much as you'll love the period decor, you'll also enjoy the modern pool, decks, and amenities.

Food

Louisville has a remarkable food scene that is constantly evolving. Many of Louisville's restaurants and chefs have received national recognition, and there is much to be impressed by. These days, downtown, especially the NuLu area, might be the most happening area, but tasty destinations abound throughout the city. The following listings make up only a small fraction of what Louisville has to offer. Ask around for favorites or hop online and visit sites such as www.hotbytes.com or http://louisville.eater.com for the latest news and reviews.

DOWNTOWN
Breakfast

Momma knew what she was talking about when she said breakfast was the most important meal of the day, so start your day right at **Toast on Market** (620 E. Market St., 502/569-4099, www.toastonmarket.com, 7am-2pm Tues.-Fri., 7am-3pm Sat.-Sun., $5.75-9.75). The King French Toast, a tribute to Elvis with its peanut butter and bananas, will get you singing, while Cliffie's Plate, involving eggs, meat, hash brown casserole, and pancakes, makes eating the rest of the day optional.

Coffee Shops

Pick up a pick-me-up in the form of a coffee drink, a baked good, or a vinyl record at **Please & Thank You** (800 E. Market St., www.pleaseandthankyoulouisville.com, 7am-6pm Mon.-Fri., 9am-6pm Sat., 9am-4pm Sun.), a small shop that is part coffee shop, part record store.

Cafés

Though they bill themselves as an "Appalachian tea and hooch café"—probably haven't been to one of those, have you?—**Hillbilly Tea** (120 S. 1st St., 502/587-7350, http://hillbillytea.com, 10am-9pm Tues.-Thurs., 10am-11pm Fri.-Sat., 10am-4pm Sun., $8-18) also serves some mighty fine food, including a very popular

brunch. Try the moonshine pork ribs, French toast with sweet grass syrup, braised lamb on succotash, or buttermilk fried quail with corn pone pudding.

If you're in the mood for a good sandwich—hearty bread, crisp vegetables, savory meats, and tasty dressings with a nice atmosphere on the side—head to **The Café** (712 Brent St., 502/589-9191, http://thecafe.ws, 7am-4pm Mon.-Sat., $5.95-8.95). The very large sandwiches are served with a choice of fresh sides; try the bean salad. For breakfast, choose from baked goods or the heartier biscuits and gravy, twice-baked French toast, or Southern grits scramble.

Casual American

If you get hungry while museum-hopping downtown, make the short walk to **Dish on Market** (434 W. Market St., 502/315-0669, http://dishonmarket.com, 8am-10pm Mon.-Thurs., 8am-midnight Fri.-Sat., 8am-8pm Sun., $6.50-10.75), where everyone in the family should find something to satisfy them. Dish offers a huge selection of salads, burgers, and sandwiches, as well as entrées of fried chicken, fish and chips, and the like. Additionally, breakfast is served daily until 2pm, and they have a bakery where you can grab pastries or sweet treats.

Play a game of table tennis or just relax with a drink at the funky **Garage Bar** (700 E. Market St., 502/749-7100, www.garageonmarket.com, 5pm-10pm Mon.-Wed., 5pm-11pm Thurs., 4pm-midnight Fri., 11am-midnight Sat., 11am-10pm Sun., $11-16), a restaurant in a converted garage that focuses on pizza. Local ingredients, including house-made sausage and pepperoni and herbs grown right out front, top the pies, and should you just want to nibble, Garage Bar also boasts a country ham and oyster bar.

Don't let the basement location discourage you from a meal at **Hammerheads** (921

THERESA DOWELL BLACKINTON

The sign at Garage Bar makes it clear what they're all about.

Swan St., 502/365-1112, www.louisvilleham-merheads.com, 5pm-10pm Mon.-Sat., $7-14), where you can get unique spins on some comforting favorites. Sink your teeth into a burger (standard beef or elk, venison, or chorizo), a taco (pork, brisket, duck, or soft shell crab), a sandwich (maybe the pork belly BLT), or the signature sweet potato waffle with chicken wings.

Contemporary American

With its clean lines and white-and-black decor, **Relish** (1346 River Rd., 502/587-7007, www.relishlouisville.com, lunch 11am-3pm Mon.-Sat., dinner 5pm-9pm Mon.-Thurs., 5pm-10pm Fri.-Sat., $12-26) has a modern Euro feel, and the food is forward-looking as well. Mindful eating is the mission behind the dishes, which include small plates, such as flatbread with lamb, mint, pomegranate molasses, and feta, and main plates, such as Asian-style salmon. A gourmet-to-go menu makes for excellent picnics. For lunch ($8.50-12), try a salad or sandwich.

The chefs at **Rye** (900 E. Market, 502/749-6200, http://ryeonmarket.com, 5pm-11pm Sun.-Thurs., 5pm-midnight Fri.-Sat., $20-32), who sharpened their knives at Tom Colicchio's Craft, use sustainable and seasonable ingredients to create outstanding dishes, such as a carrot and cantaloupe gazpacho and a Florida red grouper with curry-coconut nage and mango. Enjoy the back porch in season; otherwise watch the action in the kitchen from the elegant interior.

Locals are thankful the chef at ◖ **Decca** (812 E. Market St., 502/749-8128, http://deccarestaurant.com, 5:30pm-10pm Mon.-Thurs., 5:30pm-11pm Fri.-Sat., $14-27) decided to make the move from California to Kentucky, bringing the city an outstanding menu with such treats as diver scallop crudo, ricotta *cavatelli* with braised rabbit, wood grilled broccoli, and made-from-scratch ice cream sandwiches. Cozy up on the plush banquette in the 1870s building or snag a courtyard seat in good weather.

With most of their food coming from within 100 miles and a restaurant decked out with former church pews and large artistic photos of the farmers who grow the food, ◖ **Harvest** (624 E. Market St., 502/384-9090, www.harvestlouisville.com, lunch 11am-2:30pm Tues.-Fri., 10am-2:30pm Sat., dinner 5pm-10pm Tues.-Thurs., 5pm-11pm Fri.-Sat., brunch 11am-2:30pm Sun., $15-24) treats diners to an upscale rustic experience that is constantly changing. Try the Kentucky menu, where you might find beer cheese made with a local brew, pork loin with sweet potato grits, or johnny-cake with smoked vegetable ragout. The lunch menu features sandwiches and pizza ($12-16).

As innovative as the hotel in which it is located, 21C's **Proof on Main** (702 W. Main St., 502/217-6360, www.proofonmain.com, breakfast 7am-10pm Mon.-Fri. and 7am-noon Sat.-Sun., lunch 11am-2pm Mon.-Fri., dinner 5:30pm-10pm Sun.-Thurs., 5:30pm-11pm Fri.-Sat., $22-36) transforms locally sourced food into magical dishes. The entrées are fantastic (try the enormous pork chop), but you could easily make a dinner from the starters, which

© THERESA DOWELL BLACKINTON

Rye, one of many popular restaurants in NuLu

might include cucumber gazpacho, bison carpaccio, and country ham falafel. The bold artwork for which the hotel is known continues in Proof, and the design is modern yet inviting.

The newest restaurant of Edward Lee, whose fame has extended beyond Louisville thanks to *Top Chef,* **Milkwood** (316 W. Main St., 502/584-6455, http://actorstheatre.org/milkwood, 5:30pm-10pm Tues.-Sun., $11-28) is located at Actor's Theatre, but its popularity goes far beyond the theatre crowd. The menu at this elegant restaurant focuses on small plates of comfort bar food with Asian influence as well as larger dinners, all of which changes regularly. Try a sampling of tastes, such as cured wagyu and lamb salami, octopus bacon, and rock shrimp sausage, or order the miso smothered chicken or pork shoulder with coconut rice.

French
La Coop (732 E. Market St., 502/410-2888, www.coopbistro.com, 5:30pm-10:30pm Tues.-Thurs., 5:30-11:30 Fri.-Sat., $12-24) transports you straight to the streets of Paris with its French bistro cuisine of perfectly prepared escargot, *moules,* steak *frites,* coq au vin, and cassoulet. The atmosphere is also spot-on, right down to the sidewalk seating. On Tuesdays, a three-course prix fixe menu is offered for $25.

Latin American
The smoky notes of chiles infuse the authentic Latin American food at **Mayan Café** (813 E. Market St., 502/566-0651, www.themayancafe.com, lunch 11am-2:30pm Mon.-Fri., dinner 5pm-10pm Mon.-Thurs., 5pm-10:30pm Fri.-Sat., $12-25). Start with the *salbutes* (topped corn tortillas), which have garnered acclaim since the chef's days driving a taco truck, then pick from such entrées as wild-caught fish in achiote lime sauce or *cochinita pibil,* a slow-roasted pork. Add the lima beans as a side (trust me). When the weather's nice, sidewalk seating is available.

For a quick but tasty meal, place your order at **Taco Punk** (736 E. Market St., 502/584-8226, www.tacopunk.com, 11am-8pm Mon.-Thurs., 11am-9pm Fri.-Sat., 11am-3pm Sun.,

LOUISVILLE'S CATHOLIC LEGACY

With more than 100 parishes in the Archdiocese of Louisville and more than 20,000 students attending Catholic schools in the archdiocese, the Catholic Church holds strong influence in the city, which is not surprising if you consider that many Louisvillians come from Catholic German, Irish, and French stock. Although certainly not the only faith in town—both the Southern Baptists and Presbyterians have important seminaries in the city with congregations to match, Southeast Christian Church is one of the nation's largest megachurches, and residents of nearly every faith can find a church home in Louisville—the Catholic Church has a way of injecting itself into the city's cultural life. Two of the more popular ways are Friday fish fries and parish picnics.

On Fridays in Lent, nearly every Catholic parish puts on a fish fry, where for a low price anyone is welcome to feast on a plate of fish and Southern sides (think mac 'n' cheese, green beans, and the like). Stop in at the Catholic church nearest you to find out the schedule; if they're not hosting one, they'll know where the nearest one is.

In summer, there's not a single weekend that's without a church picnic. These aren't low-key affairs, but rather big events where the beer and brats flow freely, carnival rides keep the kids happy, and booths offer the chance for you to win a cake, a tin of popcorn, or an enormous stuffed animal. One of the most popular picnics is August's St. Joseph Orphan's Picnic (2823 Frankfort Ave.), which brings volunteers from parishes all over the city together to man more than 60 booths, with all proceeds benefiting the St. Joseph Children's Home. For a schedule of picnics, visit the Archdiocese of Louisville's website (www.archlou.org).

$3.25-4.65 per taco), where you build your gourmet taco by choosing your meat from options such as chorizo and potato, pineapple pork, and Yucatan-style shrimp. Then top it with your pick of shredded cabbage, pickled onion, jalapeños, and cilantro. Housemade tortillas hold it all together.

Dessert

Only the finest natural ingredients go into the sweet treats baked daily at **Cake Flour** (909 E. Market St., 502/719-0172, www.cakeflouronmarket.com, 7am-2pm Mon., 7am-6pm Tues.-Fri., 8am-2pm Sat.-Sun.). White chocolate cheesecake, banana truffle cupcakes, and lemon tarts are just some of the tempting goodies on offer.

Though the savory menu of French-style sandwiches, soups, salads, and crepes at **Ghyslain on Market** (721 E. Market St., 502/690-8645, www.ghyslain.com, 7am-9pm daily) makes for fantastic meals, the chocolates and pastries are what really tempt. Try a chocolate caramel cup, a vanilla cheesecake, or one of the many mousses, or put together a goodie bag of truffles.

OLD LOUISVILLE
Cafés

Artisan homemade breads are still cooked in imported European ovens and the pastries are lovingly made each day at **Ermin's Bakery and Café** (1201 S. 1st St., 502/635-6960, www.erminsbakery.com, 7am-7pm Mon.-Fri., 8am-5pm Sat., 9am-3pm Sun. $3.95-6.95). Try choosing between the cinnamon roll and apple strudel for breakfast or the petit four and sin bar (a rich combination of chocolate and peanut butter) for dessert. Whatever you end up with, your sweet tooth will be satisfied. For lunch, a half sandwich of your choice with the house tomato basil soup makes a satisfying meal.

Casual American

Popular with U of L students, the **Granville Inn** (1601 S. Third St., 502/635-6475, 11am-1am daily, $3.95-7.95) is a constant competitor for the title of best burger. The signature burger is a half-pound of hand-formed beef charbroiled to order and topped with lettuce, tomato, onion, and cheese and served with a heaping side of fries. The bar serves up cheap pints of craft draft beer, and the atmosphere is that of a local joint—a bit dark, with TVs, electronic dartboards, and a pool table.

Contemporary American

If you consider yourself a gourmand, make a reservation at **☾ 610 Magnolia** (610 W. Magnolia Ave., 502/636-0783, www.610magnolia.com, Thurs.-Sat., dinner only, reservations required) and prepare to be wowed. Widely considered to be one of the best restaurants in the region, the elegant but minimalist 610 Magnolia offers a three- ($45) or four-course ($55) prix-fixe menu that changes every night, but always centers around in-season, local, organic ingredients. What exactly will end up on your plate is a surprise, but Chef Edward Lee, cooking here long before he became a household name thanks to *Top Chef,* consistently turns out sophisticated American food enhanced with global flavors. The atmosphere of this house restaurant is understated, creating an elegant and intimate setting for a special-occasion dinner.

SOUTH LOUISVILLE
Diners

If you like to talk horse racing while you eat, stop in at **Wagner's Pharmacy** (3113 S. 4th St., 502/375-3800, www.wagnerspharmacy. com, 8am-2:30pm Mon.-Fri., 8am-noon Sat. as well as Sun. during racing meets, $3.29-8.99), just across the street from Churchill Downs. Since 1922, Wagner's has been the gathering place for those in the horse industry, and inside the simple white building decorated with images of Derby winners you're likely to share the counter with jockeys, trainers, and owners. The diner-style menu is simple: Lunch is a choice between a long list of sandwiches and the daily special (roast beef on Wednesday, fried fish on Friday), while breakfast options include a selection of omelettes, à la carte pancakes, and

platters with your choice of ham, sausage, or bacon with eggs, biscuits, and potatoes.

Asian

Don't let its strip mall location mislead you. It might not look like much, but **Vietnam Kitchen** (5339 Mitscher Ave., 502/363-5154, www.vietnamkitchen.net, 11am-10pm Sun.-Tues. and Thurs., 11am-11pm Fri.-Sat., $6-13.35) is where Louisville's many Vietnamese immigrants come to be transported back home. From the staple pho (rice-noodle soup traditionally served with beef) to meat, seafood, and vegetarian stir-fry, curry, and clay-pot dishes, the taste will take you to the other side of the world. Vegetarian options abound, and the spice level of each dish can be adjusted, from benign all the way up to "Vietnam spicy."

Indian

In an unassuming strip mall locale, **DakShin** (4742 Bardstown Rd., 502/491-7412, www.my-dakshin.com, 11am-9pm daily, $5.99-10.99) surprises with its authentic taste of India. The extensive menu covers Northern Indian dishes such as *malai kofta,* lamb vindaloo, and chicken korma; Southern Indian dishes such as paneer *dosai, bagara baigan,* and Kerala fish curry; and Indo-Chinese noodle, rice, and stir-fry dishes. It's the best Indian food in town.

FRANKFORT AVENUE
Coffee Shops

A favorite place to work, study, or just relax, **Vint** (2309 Frankfort Ave., 502/894-8060, 6:30am-10pm Mon.-Wed., 6:30am-11pm Thurs.-Fri., 7:30am-11pm Sat., 8am-9pm Sun.) can satisfy your craving for coffee or beer and wine. If you're on the go, hit the drive-through.

Barbecue

The **Frankfort Avenue Beer Depot** (3204 Frankfort Ave., 502/895-3223, www.frankfortavenuebeerdepot.com, 11am-10pm, bar open until 2am daily, $5-14), is a super casual joint, basically a dive, that serves amazing brisket, ribs, chicken, and pulled pork, smoked right in the front parking lot, along with fantastic coleslaw, potato salad, baked beans, macaroni and cheese, and spicy fries. As the name suggests, there's plenty of beer on offer, and many people come by just to have a drink and play the mini-golf course out back or a round of cornhole.

Pizza
Everyone knows the crust is the key to a good pizza, and the pies at **Coal's Artisan Pizza** (3730 Frankfort Ave., 502/742-8200, http://coalsartisanpizza.com, 11:30am-10pm Mon.-Thurs., 11:30am-11pm Fri.-Sat., noon-9pm Sun., $12-15) have the perfect crust—thin, smoky, and just a little sweet. Choose a specialty pizza named for one of Louisville's neighborhoods or deck your own with gourmet ingredients like caramelized onions and piquillo peppers. The weekday lunches are a great deal.

Asian
At **⟨C⟩ Basa** (2244 Frankfort Ave., 502/896-1016, www.basarestaurant.com, 5pm-10pm Mon.-Thurs., 5pm-11pm Fri.-Sat., $15-29), a 2008 James Beard Best New Restaurant semifinalist, local ingredients are transformed into tantalizing modern Vietnamese cuisine. The menu is small and focused, with many of the appetizers and entrées featuring seafood—prawns, tuna, oysters, mussels, and the like. One of the most raved-about entrées, however, is the Shaking Beef, cubed filet mignon cooked with garlic, watercress, cherry tomatoes, and red onions in a very hot wok. Expect elegant presentation and fine service at one of Louisville's more exciting restaurants.

A longtime favorite of vegetarians, **Zen Garden** (2240 Frankfort Ave., 502/895-9114, http://zengardenasian.com, 11am-3pm and 5pm-9:30pm Mon.-Thurs., 11am-3pm and 5pm-10pm Fri., noon-10pm Sat., $7.95-10.95) serves up popular dishes such as pad Thai, udon, and various stir-fries, all sans meat. The entire menu is available for carry-out.

Don't overlook tiny but colorful **Sari Sari** (2339 Frankfort Ave., 502/894-0585, 5pm-9pm Tues. and Sat., 11:30am-9pm Wed.-Fri., $4.95-12.95), where you can get a delicious and filling meal of Filipino favorites, a cuisine that combines Asian and Latin flavors in such dishes as chicken coconut curry, pork menudo, and pork adobo.

Irish
A traditional Irish pub, the **Irish Rover** (2319 Frankfort Ave., 502/899-3544, www.theirishroverky.com, 11:30am-11pm Mon.-Thurs., 11:30am-midnight Fri.-Sat., $6.95-14.95) is where the large percentage of Louisvillians who claim Irish heritage come for a taste of the old country. The menu features such hearty standards as fish and chips, bangers and mash, smoked salmon and potato gratin, and cottage pie—a bread bowl filled with steaming Guinness beef stew and topped with mashed potatoes and cheese. You certainly won't go home hungry.

Italian
Sophisticated **Volare** (2300 Frankfort Ave., 502/894-4446, www.volare-restaurant.com, 5pm-10pm Sun.-Thurs., 5pm-11pm Fri.-Sat., $18-39) satisfies with modern Italian food that is locally sourced and house-made. You'll find favorites such as osso buco and chicken marsala as well as exciting specials. For something lighter, try the small plates at the bar, where there's live music Wednesday-Saturday.

Latin American
Neighborhood anchor **El Mundo** (2345 Frankfort Ave., 502/899-9930, www.502elmundo.com, 11:30am-10pm Tues.-Sat., $7.25-14.95) serves up Mexican food with a twist. In addition to considering the burritos, enchiladas, and other favorites, see what's on special. The fish tacos and the grilled fajitas of the day are always good choices, and the margaritas and sangria are top-notch. The two-story restaurant offers counter service downstairs and waiter service upstairs and on the patio. It's a tight space, so expect to get friendly with your neighbors and to wait if you come at peak hours.

Mediterranean
A Frankfort Avenue institution, **Grape Leaf**

(2217 Frankfort Ave., 502/897-1774, www.
grapeleafonline.com, 11am-9pm Mon.-Thurs.,
9:30am-10pm Fri.-Sat., 9:30am-9pm Sun., $11-
18.50) keeps regulars coming back for their tenderloin kabobs, moussaka, and falafel. On a
nice day, sit outside and munch from the sampler appetizer, which comes with your choice of
three items, including hummus, grape leaves,
and spanakopita.

Dessert

What is life without dessert? **Sweet Surrender
Dessert Café** (1804 Frankfort Ave., 502/899-
2008, www.sweetsurrenderdessertcafe.com,
10am-10pm Tues.-Thurs., 10am-11pm Fri.-
Sat.) certainly makes you wonder just that,
with its sinful selection of cakes, tortes, pies,
cupcakes, cookies, and dessert bars. Selection
varies, which means that if your favorite is un-
available, you'll just have to come up with a
new favorite. It's not hard to do.

You can stick with the tried-and-true at **The
Comfy Cow** (2221 Frankfort Ave., 502/409-
4616, http://thecomfycow.com, 11am-10pm

Sun.-Thurs., 11am-11pm Fri.-Sat.) and you'll
be more than happy, but this impossible-to-
miss bright pink ice cream parlor churns out
an impressive array of original flavors. Why not
try dulce de leche de salte, bourbon ball, or
Vermont maple walnut? No pick is a bad pick.

EAST LOUISVILLE
Breakfast

As you'd expect from the name, you can get
eggs any way you want them—served Tex-
Mex or Benedict style, in omelettes or bur-
ritos, in scrambles or skillets—at **Wild Eggs**
(3985 Dutchmans Ln., 502/893-8005, www.
crackinwildeggs.com, 6:30am-2:30pm Mon.-
Fri., 7am-3pm Sat.-Sun., $4.50-11.95). If the
thought of eggs isn't making you go wild, then
choose from a variety of other breakfast favorites, like stuffed French toast or variations on
pancakes, waffles, and crepes.

Casual American

Located at Harrods Creek on the Ohio River,
Captain's Quarters (5700 Captain's Quarters

The Comfy Cow, a favorite ice cream destination

© THERESA DOWELL BLACKINTON

Rd., 502/228-1651, www.cqriverside.com, 11:30am-10pm Mon.-Thurs., 11:30am-11pm Fri.-Sat., 10:30am-10pm Sun., $7.95-17.95) is Louisville's go-to restaurant for casual riverside dining. Though the dining room is bright and spacious with windows providing water views, it's the multilevel deck overlooking the river that attracts people to Captain's Quarters. As you might expect, the menu is heavy on seafood, offering fried cod, pan-seared salmon, seafood tortellini, and more, in addition to sandwiches, pizzas, and chicken and beef entrées. The fried banana peppers are a favorite of the happy hour crowd. Captain's Quarters offers tie-ups for hungry or thirsty boaters.

Asian

Whether you want pineapple fried rice, *pad kee mow,* or *massaman* curry, **Simply Thai** (323 Wallace Ave., 502/899-9670, www.simplythaiky.com, lunch 11am-2:30pm Mon.-Fri. and noon-3pm Sat., dinner 4:30pm-9:30pm Mon.-Thurs., 4:30pm-10:30pm Fri., 5pm-10:30pm Sat., $9-17) will satisfy. Portions are large and presentation is not overlooked at this small restaurant full of flavorful dishes.

Latin American

Rather than the usual Tex-Mex more common to the area, **C Guaca Mole** (9921 Ormsby Station Rd., 502/365-4822, 11am-9:30pm Mon.-Thurs., 11am-10pm Fri., noon-10pm Sat., noon-8:30pm Sun., $8-16), a Mexican cantina-style restaurant, focuses on more authentic dishes, including melt-in-your-mouth carnitas, chicken *tinga sopes,* and short rib *enfrijolades.* You'll even find proper moles as well as seviche.

Since most of us can't legally travel to Cuba, the best we can do to get a taste of the bright flavors of that forbidden Caribbean island is have a meal at **Havana Rumba** (4115 Oechsli Ave., 502/897-1959, http://havanarumbaonline.com, 5pm-9:30pm Mon.-Wed., 11am-9:30pm Thurs., 11am-10pm Fri., noon-10pm Sat., noon-8:30pm Sun., $7.50-15.99), where the Cuban-born chef-owner dishes up an extensive menu of family recipes in a warm, festive atmosphere. Try the *papas rellenos* (mashed potato balls filled with seasoned ground beef), the Cubano sandwich, or the *lechon asado.*

BARDSTOWN ROAD AREA
Coffee Shops

Day's Espresso & Coffee (1420 Bardstown Rd., 502/456-1170, www.dayscoffee.com, 6:30am-10pm Mon.-Thurs., 6:30am-11pm Fri.-Sat.) claims to have the finest cappuccino in town, and customers declare the iced latte to be unbeatable. Without pretension, Day's is friendly, and service is good.

Heine Brothers (2200 Bardstown Rd., 502/515-0380, www.heinebroscoffee.com, 6:30am-10pm Mon.-Thurs., 6:30am-11pm Fri.-Sat., 7am-10pm Sun., $2-5), Louisville's neighborhood coffee shop, serves the coffee that keeps the Derby City chugging. Having cofounded a first-of-its-kind organic, fair-trade, and green coffee co-op as well as a nonprofit that turns coffee grounds into compost, Heine Bros. isn't just good for a pick-me-up—it's also good for your soul. Multiple outposts are located around town, welcoming you to bring a book, a computer, or a friend and hang out for as long as you like.

Highland Coffee (1140 Bardstown Rd., 502/451-4545, www.highlandcoffeelouisville.com, 6am-10pm Mon.-Wed., 6am-11pm Thurs., 6am-midnight Fri., 6:30am-midnight Sat., 6:30am-10pm Sun.), which draws a young, artsy crowd, claims to be "keeping Louisville wired" with their selection of coffee drinks and baked goods. Breakfast wraps are available in the morning, and panini are made fresh later in the day.

Contemporary American

Exuberant is the best way to describe **Café Lou Lou** (2216 Dundee Rd., 502/459-9566, www.cafeloulou.com, 11am-10pm Sun.-Thurs., 11am-11pm Fri.-Sat., $9-16), a fun and funky favorite with bold decor, spunky servers, and creative food. Though at first glance, the menu seems strongly Italian/Mediterranean thanks to its wide selection of pastas and pizzas, a closer look will reveal the chef's Louisiana and Louisville connections. Pasta jambalaya, muffuletta sandwiches, and Hot Brown pizzas share space with Italian meatball calzones, spinach and tomato crispy lavash, and blue cheese polenta.

◖ Jack Fry's (1007 Bardstown Rd., 502/452-9244, www.jackfrys.com, lunch 11am-2:30pm Mon.-Fri., dinner 5:30pm-11pm Mon.-Thurs., 5:30pm-midnight Fri.-Sat., 5:30pm-10pm Sun., $21-43) is an anchor of the Louisville restaurant scene, pleasing regulars and newcomers alike with its upscale American cuisine, with hints of Southern and French flavors, served in a warm bistro setting. Appetizers range from the signature shrimp and grits to foie gras, while entrées include lamb chops, filet, and herb-brined chicken. Presentation and service are top-notch. Those on a budget should check out the lunch menu ($12-16).

Long before it was the cool thing to do, **Lilly's** (1147 Bardstown Rd., 502/451-0477, www.lillyslapeche.com, 11am-3pm and 5pm-10pm Tues.-Sat., $14-32) established an award-winning menu based almost exclusively on locally sourced food. That means the beet and arugula salad, the housemade lobster agnolotti, and the pulled Moroccan lamb shoulder are bursting with fresh flavor. The menu changes seasonally, but you're guaranteed to find local food transformed into refined dishes influenced by international flavors at this Kentucky bistro.

Barbecue

In the tradition of good barbecue restaurants, **Mark's Feed Store** (1514 Bardstown Rd., 502/458-1570, www.marksfeedstore.com, 11am-10pm Sun.-Thurs., 11am-11pm Fri.-Sat., $7.29-16.59) keeps things simple. Choose among pork, beef, or chicken sandwiches or platters or a rack of fall-off-the-bone ribs. Everything's hickory smoked and, in Kentucky barbecue style, doused with thick and slightly spicy sauce. Sides are what you'd expect: spicy fries, coleslaw, baked apples, baked beans, and the like.

Asian

The cooking as well as the decor is bright and crisp at **Asiatique** (1767 Bardstown Rd., 502/451-2749, www.asiatiquerestaurant.com, 5pm-10pm Mon.-Thurs., 5pm-11pm Fri., noon-3pm and 5pm-11pm Sat., 4pm-10pm Sun. $18-28), an upscale Pacific Rim restaurant with a global view. Malaysian-born Chef Looi, who has been a guest chef at the James Beard Foundation three times, turns out well-executed and mouthwatering cuisine, which changes seasonally, though favorites like the wok-seared salmon usually aren't off the menu for long. Five-course tasting menus are also offered nightly.

Dragon King's Daughter (1126 Bardstown Rd., 602/632-2444, www.dragonkingsdaughter.com, 3pm-11pm Mon.-Wed., noon-midnight Thurs.-Sat., noon-10pm Sun., $8-12) gets creative with sushi, tempura, teriyaki, and other Japanese dishes. For example, you can order a sashimi pizza, made with long strips of red tuna, white tuna, and salmon laid on top of mixed greens and placed on a piece of flatbread dressed with Japanese mayo, or tacos with shrimp tempura, Asian barbecue beef, or chicken katsu. Regular sushi rolls are also available in this casual—and sometimes noisy—storefront restaurant. The happy hour menu (3pm-6pm and 10pm-midnight daily) is a good deal.

Vietnamese sandwiches are the focus at **Banh Mi Hero** (2245 Bardstown Rd., 502/456-2022, http://bahnmihero.com, 11am-9pm Mon.-Thurs., 11am-10pm Fri.-Sat., $4-8), where traditional and unique takes on *banh mi* are made with fresh bread, homemade pâté, house aioli, fresh veggies, and quality meats. Warning: *Banh mi* can be addictive.

International

Ramsi's Café on the World (1293 Bardstown Rd., 502/451-0700, www.ramsiscafe.com, 11am-1am Mon.-Thurs., 11am-2am Fri.-Sat., 10am-11pm Sun., $9-22) isn't kidding about the "world" part. Although Ramsi and his family hail from Lebanon, their restaurant serves up dishes from all over the map (as well as ingredients from their own farm), and they aren't afraid to mix and match the best of what the world has to offer. The East Meets South Fajitas, for instance, take traditional fajita ingredients and wrap them in Indian paratha bread, while the ribs are served with a Caribbean-style mango sauce. Vegetarians, vegans, and those with gluten allergies are generously catered for. Expect enormous portions, an eclectic and friendly staff, and very possibly a wait thanks to all the loyal patrons.

Latin American
Named for the trendy neighborhood in Buenos Aires, **Palermo Viejo** (1359 Bardstown Rd., 502/456-6461, 5pm-11pm Mon.-Sat., $12-17) serves up the tasty steaks (plus *chimichurri*) for which Argentina is known. True meat lovers can indulge in the *parrillada*, a mixed grill of chorizo, short ribs, tenderloin, and sweetbreads. Order a side of the parsley and garlic fries to complete your meal. In a nod to other popular Argentinean cuisine, the menu also offers empanadas and a selection of pasta. In summer, when you can sit outdoors and people watch, the small restaurant gains a few seats.

Garnering national recognition for its Nuevo Latino cuisine, including multiple James Beard nominations, **[** **Seviche** (1538 Bardstown Rd., 502/473-8560, www.sevicherestaurant.com, 5pm-10pm Mon.-Thurs., 5pm-11pm Fri.-Sat., 5pm-9pm Sun., $19-25) entices diners with its namesake seviches and its tightly curated entrée list. Those who can't choose between the big-eye tuna seviche with coconut and lemongrass and the wild-caught shrimp with chipotle can opt for a seviche tasting of three or five options. Although the way each dish is served changes with the season, entrée options usually include multiple seafood plates as well as chicken and steak. With a creative menu,

warm atmosphere, ample outdoor seating, and excellent service, what's not to like?

Mediterranean
Take it from a girl who spent a year in Greece eating gyros every day—**Zaytun** (2286 Bardstown Rd., 502/365-1788, 11:30am-10pm Mon.-Thurs., 11:30am-11pm Fri.-Sat., noon-9pm Sun., $7.95-11.95) has the best gyros in town. The pita isn't traditional, more of a flatbread instead, but it's delicious, and the meat (choose between chicken or a mix of lamb and beef) is seasoned, cooked, and cut just right.

Dessert
At **Homemade Ice Cream and Pie Kitchen** (2525 Bardstown Rd., 502/459-8184, www.piekitchen.com, 7am-10pm Sun.-Thurs., 7am-11pm Fri.-Sat.), they don't mislead you with their name. The scrumptious homemade ice cream, pie, and other desserts are what have kept Louisvillians coming in for more than a quarter century (when what was a lunch counter became dessert heaven thanks to its oft-requested pies). The caramel-iced Dutch apple pie and the seasonal pumpkin ice cream win raves, but the kitchen probably makes a delicious version of whatever flavor is your favorite. If you've been really good, reward yourself with a combo of the store's two namesake dishes: ice cream pie. Multiple other locations are scattered throughout town.

Legend has it that Elizabeth Kizito of **Kizito Cookies** (1398 Bardstown Rd., 502/456-2891, www.kizito.com, 7am-5pm Tues.-Fri., 8am-5pm Sat.) was born under a banana tree, then learned to bake from her father in Africa before immigrating to the United States at age 17. Whether that's true or not, Kizito cookies are certainly legendary in their own right. Big enough to share and perfectly chewy, the cookies come in 12 different flavors. Stick with traditional chocolate chip or try the pecan-and-chocolate Lucky in Kentucky; it's impossible to go wrong.

Information and Transportation

INFORMATION

The **Louisville Visitors Center** (301 S. 4th St., 502/379-6109, www.gotolouisville.com, 10am-5pm Mon.-Sat., noon-5pm Sun.), located between the Kentucky International Convention Center and Fourth Street Live!, offers advice, maps, reservations, brochures, and everything else you need to arrange your visit.

If you're downtown and looking to mail a postcard home, the 4th Street **post office** (411 S. 4th St., 9am-5pm weekdays) is most central.

The *Courier-Journal* (www.courierjournal.com), Kentucky's largest newspaper, is published daily in Louisville. *LEO Weekly* (www.leoweekly.com) is the city's alternative newspaper and the source for what's happening around town. You can pick it up free at restaurants, bars, shops, and stands around the city.

GETTING THERE

Air

Although UPS is the only carrier flying internationally from the amusingly named **Louisville International Airport** (600 Terminal Dr., 502/368-6524, www.flylouisville.com)—still referred to by many locals as Standiford Field (the former name and the source of airport code SDF)—you can't find many other faults with the airport. It's conveniently located only about five miles south of downtown, and it's notably simple to navigate, with two terminals, each branching off from the main hall and each easily reached on foot. Airlines offer nonstop flights to 20 destinations and a slew of connecting flights to cities around the world. To get to or from the airport, you can take a taxi, rental car, hotel shuttle, or bus.

TARC Route 2 runs between downtown, Old Louisville, and the airport. The bus runs from about 6am to about 10pm daily, with the trip taking about 20 minutes to Old Louisville and 30 minutes to downtown. Buses depart every 40-90 minutes depending on the day and time. Adult fare is $1.75. Check the schedule at www.ridetarc.org.

Bus

Greyhound services Louisville with a downtown station (720 W. Muhammad Ali Blvd., 502/561-2805, www.greyhound.com).

Car

Lying at the intersections of I-65, I-64, and I-71, Louisville is easily accessed by car from north, south, east, and west. If you're coming from within the state, Louisville is 40 miles (45 minutes) from Bardstown via northbound I-65, 80 miles (1.5 hours) from Lexington via westbound I-64, 100 miles (1.5 hours) from Covington via southbound I-71, 195 miles (3 hours) from Ashland via westbound I-64, 110 miles (2 hours) from Owensboro via northbound U.S. 231 and eastbound I-64, and 220 miles (3.25 hours) from Paducah via U.S. 9001 and northbound I-65.

From out-of-state locations, Louisville is 260 miles (4 hours) east of St. Louis via I-64, 115 miles (1.75 hours) south of Indianapolis via I-65, 100 miles (1.5 hours) southwest of Cincinnati via I-71, and 175 miles (2.5 hours) north of Nashville via I-65.

GETTING AROUND

Car Rental

Your best bet for exploring Louisville, especially if you want to go beyond downtown, is to rent a car. **Advantage** (800/777-5500, www.advantage.com), **Alamo** (800/462-5266, www.alamo.com), **Avis** (800/331-1212, www.avis.com), **Budget** (800/527-0700, www.budget.com), **Dollar** (800/800-3665, www.dollar.com), **Enterprise** (800/261-7331, www.enterprise.com), **Hertz** (800/654-3131, www.hertz.com), **National** (877/222-9058, www.nationalcar.com), and **Thrifty** (888/400-8877, www.thrifty.com) all have desks at the airport. Cars can be reserved online through the companies' national websites.

Metered street parking is available downtown with limits of 1-4 hours. All meters take coins, and the newer meters also take credit cards. Parking is free on the streets after 6pm and on Sundays. The city runs six lots and 14 garages, most of which have an all-day rate of $5 or $10, with hourly rates also available. Look for blue PARC signs to identify these parking areas.

Bus

Public transportation within Louisville is offered by **TARC** (www.ridetarc.org), the Transit Authority of the River City, and is limited to buses and trolleys. Getting across town via bus is not a particularly efficient way of travel, but the Main-Market and Fourth Street trolleys cover nearly all of downtown's tourist sites. Use the "Plan Your Trip" feature on TARC's website to determine your options. Bus fare is $1.75 for adults, $0.80 for students, seniors, and riders with disabilities. Transfers are free. Trolley rides are free. A Day Tripper pass offers unlimited rides on the day of purchase for $3.50 and can be purchased at the Louisville Visitors Center.

Taxi

Although it's not too difficult to flag down a taxi in the city center, it's almost always easier and safer to call and order a cab. All hotels and many restaurants and sights will arrange a taxi for you; just ask at the concierge, hostess, or information desk. Cabs in Louisville are metered with rates set by the city. Taxi options include **Green Cab** (502/635-6400), **Yellow Cab** (502/636-5511), and **AAA Taxi Cab** (502/225-4901).

Pedicabs and Horse Trams

If you're looking for an alternative way of getting from point A to point B, hop in one of the bright red vehicles operated by **Derby City Pedicabs** (502/338-0877, www.derbycitypedicabs.com), most often found near Fourth Street Live!, Slugger Field, Waterfront Park, and along Bardstown Road. Drivers work for tips only, so you decide the fare. Don't be cheap; it's not easy to pedal passengers around town, and the drivers do their best to make the ride fun.

If elegant is more your style, then opt to see downtown Louisville from an old-fashioned carriage crafted by Amish artisans and pulled by majestic draft horses on a ride with **Louisville Horse Trams** (502/581-0100, www.louisvillehorsetrams.com). A standard 30-minute ride for up to three people costs $40, with prices going up from there depending on length of trip and number of people. You can often find the carriages out on the town, especially on summer weekends and near Waterfront Park.

Tours

If you'd rather leave the planning to someone else, contact **Mint Julep Tours** (866/986-8779, www.mintjuleptours.com, from $59) to sign up for their Historic Louisville Tour, which hits city highlights downtown, along the Ohio River, and in Old Louisville. They also offer Bourbon Trail and Horse Country tours and can customize a tour especially for you.

LOUISVILLE

Vicinity of Louisville

For day excursions, you have a number of options. You can head southwest to Fort Knox to get a dose of military history, southeast to Taylorsville to enjoy a day at the lake, or east to Shelbyville to visit standardbred horse farms.

FORT KNOX AND MEADE COUNTY

Located south of Louisville, Fort Knox is a city-size army base with a population of 23,000 soldiers and civilians located in Meade County, which is also home to the wonderful Otter Creek Outdoor Recreation Area. As you approach Fort Knox, don't be surprised to hear the thunder of tanks, as Fort Knox is home to the U.S. Armor Center and School and is the training grounds for the M1 Abrams Main Battle Tank used by both the Army and the Marines. Additionally, as one of five basic combat training facilities in the nation, Fort Knox sees a constant stream of new recruits pass through its gates.

To the general public, Fort Knox is most well known as the home of the U.S. Bullion Depository, or in lay terms, the Gold Vault. Its aura of impenetrability has introduced Fort Knox into the popular vernacular, and it has appeared in many movies such as the James Bond flick *Goldfinger*. Unfortunately, without a presidential order, the vault, which contains more than 5,000 tons of gold, is as inaccessible as claimed, but Fort Knox itself is open to visitors.

Sights

For military buffs, the **General George Patton Museum** (4554 Fayette Ave., 502/624-3812, www.generalpatton.org, 9am-4:30pm Tues.-Fri., 10am-5:30pm Sat., free) is a must-see. Established shortly after the end of World War II, the museum has two main focuses: artifacts related to General George S. Patton Jr. and mechanized cavalry and armory. Unless

you're a member of the armed forces, you probably won't get a more up-close look at armored vehicles dating back to 1917. And for fans of Old Blood and Guts, this museum is where you come to pay tribute to the man, the myth, and the legend.

Recreation

Consisting of 2,600 gorgeous acres of wild space, **Otter Creek Outdoor Recreation Area** (KY 1638, Brandenburg, 502/942-9171, http://fw.ky.gov, dawn-dusk Wed.-Sun.) abounds with outdoor opportunities: hiking, mountain biking, horseback riding, fishing, boating, picnicking, and wildlife watching. It also features archery and shooting ranges and a disc golf course. Hunting is allowed in season. For those wishing to stay overnight, a campground ($12-20) offers sites for tents, RVs, and those with horses. There is a $3 entry fee for all visitors 12 and older and an additional $7 permit fee for use of horse trails, mountain bike trails, and the archery and shooting ranges.

Getting There and Around

Fort Knox is located 35 miles (45 minutes) south of Louisville, off of U.S. 31. All vehicles and visitors are subject to search, and weapons are not permitted on base. To reach Otter Creek, take U.S. 31W to KY 1638.

TAYLORSVILLE LAKE

Stretching through three counties and covering 3,050 acres, Taylorsville Lake is the closest destination to Louisville for water recreation. The fishing is good here, whether you're looking to cast for bluegill and sunfish along the shore or are angling to land a bass. Skiing, swimming, and other water sports are also popular. Built in the 1960s by the U.S. Army Corps of Engineers to control flooding, Taylorsville Lake is surrounded by 12,093 acres of protected land used for wildlife management as well as recreation.

Whether you wish to get out on the water or explore land-based activities, you'll want to base yourself at Taylorsville Lake State Park.

Recreation

Located right on the water, **Taylorsville Lake State Park** (2825 Overlook Rd., 502/477-8713, http://parks.ky.gov, free) draws anglers, water skiers, personal watercraft users, and pleasure boaters looking for a day in the sun. The park maintains four boat ramps that are free and accessible to the public. If you don't have your own watercraft, the **Taylorsville Marina** (1240 Settlers Trace Rd., 502/477-8766, www.taylorsvillelakemarina.com) will set you up for the day. You can rent pontoons, deck boats, and jon boats by the day.

Beyond the lake, the park encompasses 1,200 acres of forest and field. The 24-mile trail system is a favorite for horseback riding, though it's officially a mixed-use trail also open to mountain bikers and hikers. During wet periods, the horses can really tear up the trail, so if you're looking to hike, check conditions before you lace up your boots. The trails are particularly nice in autumn when the trees are ablaze with color and the weather is mild.

Accommodations

Edgewater Resort (1238 Settlers Trace Rd., 502/477-9196, www.edgewatertaylorsville-lake.com, $189-299), the only development on Taylorsville Lake, offers fully furnished cottages complete with decks with hot tubs. The majority of the cottages sleep four, though some can accommodate up to eight guests—perfect for a family vacation. From the cottages, a series of paths provide access to the lake, while boaters can launch their craft from a nearby ramp. A beach area has been created for resort guests, and Edgewater also offers trail bikes, canoe rentals, and guided boat excursions.

Geared toward RV campers, the **Taylorsville Lake Campground** (1320 Park Rd., 502/477-8713, http://parks.ky.gov) is open year-round and has 45 large sites with full hookups ($25). In a nod to the park's popularity with horse lovers, 10 additional sites are designated for horse camping ($27), and there are 15 primitive tent sites ($18). All campers share a central service building that includes laundry facilities.

Food

Aside from a selection of pizza, sandwiches, and burgers sold at the Taylorsville Marina, no food vendors operate in the park. Bring what you need with you or stock up at **Settlers Trace Grocery & Deli** (25 Overlook Rd., 502/477-9676, 5am-8pm Mon.-Sat., 7am-7pm Sun.), which is right up the road from the marina.

Getting There and Around

Taylorsville Lake State Park is located about 20 miles (30 minutes) southeast of the intersection of I-265 and I-64. From Louisville, take eastbound I-64 to Taylorsville Road (Exit 32A) and then follow signs to the lake and park entrances.

SHELBYVILLE

Known as the Saddlebred Capital of the World, Shelbyville is to equestrian events what Lexington is to thoroughbred horse farms. In fact, the eminence of the Shelbyville horse farms helped Kentucky land the 2010 World Equestrian Games, an international competition that had never before taken place outside of Europe.

Beyond its horse farms, Shelbyville is a friendly small town with a center that begs you to get out of your car and explore it on foot. Main and Washington Streets are particularly pedestrian-friendly with a slew of storefronts selling antiques, art, and home decor.

Sights

Though none of Shelbyville's American saddlebred horse farms have regularly scheduled hours for visits from the public, the **Shelbyville Visitors Bureau** (800/680-6388) organizes tours of a working farm. Tours last 60-90 minutes and occur year-round, though you'll need to make reservations two or three days ahead of your visit. If you stay at a local hotel, the tour is free, and your hotel can help with the arrangements. For those not overnighting in Shelbyville, tours cost $6 for adults and $3 for youth 5-12.

For a taste (both literal and figurative) of farm life, locals swear there isn't a better place in the area than **Gallrein Farms** (1029 Vigo Rd., 502/633-4849, www.gallreinfarms. com, 9am-6pm Mon.-Sat., 1pm-5pm Sun.), especially if you have kids. The farm is open spring through fall and contains a produce market as well as a petting zoo and duck pond loved by both the young and the young at heart. Spring and summer offer berry picking, while fall is particularly popular thanks to horse-drawn wagon rides, pumpkin picking, and a corn maze.

Shopping
Antiques hunters seek out Shelbyville's **Wakefield-Scearce Galleries** (525 Washington St., 502/633-4382, www.wakefieldscearce. com, 10am-5pm Mon.-Sat.), which has 32,000 square feet of showrooms dedicated to English antiques. Even if you aren't in the market for any of the amazing pieces on sale here, stop in to browse the impressive collection of antique silver, paintings, furniture, and other home accessories.

Recreation
Favored by bass anglers, the 325-acre **Guist Creek Lake** (11990 Boat Dock Rd., 502/647-5359, www.guistcreek.com, $5 launch fee) also contains catfish, crappie, and bluegill, and it's a rare day when you can't find a quiet spot to cast your line. For those without their own boat, 14-foot jon boats are available for rent at the marina, which also stocks tackle, boat gear, fuel, food, and drinks. From the end of May to the end of September, water skiing is allowed in a specially designated area. For those who like to do some night fishing or who want to make a weekend of it, a campground is open March-November with both tent ($17) and pull-through ($20) sites.

Accommodations
Many people visit Shelbyville on a day trip and spend the night in either Louisville or Frankfort because the options in Shelbyville are limited, though the usual chain hotel suspects do exist.

In nearby Simpsonville, which lies between Louisville and Shelbyville, the **Yellow Carriage House** (4876 Shelbyville Rd., 502/376-9754, www.yellowcarriagehouse.com, $159) is a secluded bed-and-breakfast surrounded by horse fields. Choose between the King and Queen suites in the main house, each with marble shower and private balcony or veranda, or elect for the separate Carriage House, where the candlelight breakfast available to all guests is delivered straight to your room on a silver platter.

Food
Turns out it wasn't just the Colonel who could cook. At **Claudia Sanders Dinner House** (3202 Shelbyville Rd., 502/633-5600, www. claudiasanders.com, 11am-9pm Tues.-Sun., $8.99-18.95), you can choose from a long list of Kentucky specialties straight from the cookbook of Mrs. Colonel Sanders. Though fried chicken and country ham take up a prime portion of the menu, you can also select steaks, chops, fish, and seafood, as well as salads and sandwiches. Dinner is served with family-style sides and a bread bowl that never empties, and of course, all meals are served with a heavy helping of Southern hospitality.

For a pick-me-up, stop in at **Sixth and Main Coffee House** (547 Main St., 502/647-7751, www.6amcoffee.com, 7am-6pm Mon.-Sat., 8am-1pm Sun.), where the brightly colored walls and expertly brewed coffee drinks will get you going again. If you'd rather relax, grab a book from the shelf running the length of the café or just watch out the window as small-town life occurs.

Get friendly with the locals at the monthly **Lake Shelby Fish Fry** (717 Burks Branch Rd., 502/633-5059, www.shelbycountyparks.com), held 5pm-7:30pm on the third Friday of the month May-September. For $8.50, you'll get a heaping plate of fish, coleslaw, hush puppies, and potato wedges, as well as ice cream for dessert and your choice of tea or lemonade. The conversation is free.

Not quite in town but just a few miles away, Simpsonville's **Old Stone Inn** (6905 Shelbyville Rd., 502/722-8200, www.old-stone-inn.com, 4pm-10pm Mon.-Sat., $14-27) is worth the trip. This limestone building from the early 1800s has seen life as a stagecoach stop as well as a tavern and inn, though it's been operating as a restaurant since 1920. Enjoy the warm ambience created by the four original fireplaces while feasting on elegantly plated Southern favorites like country ham, shrimp and grits, and chicken livers. When the weather's nice, take advantage of happy hour on the patio complete with live local music.

Getting There and Around

From Louisville, Shelbyville is an easy 30-mile (40-minute) drive straight east on I-64. You can continue east on I-64 to both Frankfort (25 miles, 35 minutes) and Lexington (50 miles, one hour).

BARDSTOWN, THE BOURBON TRAIL, AND FRANKFORT

The spirit of Kentucky flows out of the central region that includes Bardstown, the Bourbon Trail, and Frankfort. For some, this spirit is religious. Bardstown is Kentucky's holy land, home to the first Catholic diocese in the West. Today, multiple religious orders base themselves here, and landmark religious sites draw the faithful. For many more, however, the spirit they think of when the towns of this region spring to mind is amber-colored and comes in a bottle. Here in central Kentucky, the world's best bourbon—America's only native spirit—is distilled, bottled, and aged.

The locations featured in this chapter are not cities; they're towns. Even Frankfort, the unassuming capital of Kentucky, is no more than a large town. You can explore each and every destination on foot, strolling down revitalized Main Streets lined with historic buildings hosting restaurants, B&Bs, and shops as you make your way from site to site. Expect people to say hello, to ask where you're from, to point out their favorite places. This is small-town America, where festivals are still begun with parades, where neighbors are never strangers, and where the best cooking is home cooking.

Leave each of the towns that dot the route between Bardstown and Frankfort, and you'll find yourself amid farmland. The limestone layer that makes the water so fine for bourbon is good for growing things, too. Weathered barns, tall silos, bright green fields, and large herds of cattle or other livestock enhance the scenery as you travel from distillery to distillery. Many of the distilleries themselves are located essentially on farmland; the warehouses

HIGHLIGHTS

LOOK FOR ◖ TO FIND RECOMMENDED SIGHTS, ACTIVITIES, DINING, AND LODGING.

BARDSTOWN

◖ **My Old Kentucky Home State Park:** Take a tour of the Federal-style home that inspired Stephen Foster to write what would become Kentucky's state song (page 73).

◖ **Kentucky Bourbon Festival:** Meet master distillers, sip premium bourbons, and celebrate American's native spirit (page 76).

◖ **Abraham Lincoln Birthplace and Boyhood Home:** Walk in the footsteps of young Abe Lincoln at the sites where he spent his formative years in what was then the American frontier (page 82).

◖ **Bernheim Arboretum:** Immerse yourself in natural beauty while hiking, fishing, or admiring a variety of gardens (page 86).

◖ **Maker's Mark Distillery:** Watch as workers hand-dip bottles of Maker's Mark in the signature red wax on a tour of this idyllic distillery (page 87).

◖ **Thomas D. Clark Center for Kentucky History:** Trace the history of Kentucky back through thousands of years by way of interactive exhibits and performances (page 97).

◖ **Buffalo Trace Distillery:** Passionate guides make for an excellent tour that concludes with a tasting of your choice of spirits (page 99).

where barrels of bourbon age are easy to pick out once you know what you're looking for.

One of the most idyllic regions of Kentucky, as well as the area attracting the most new tourists, Bardstown, the Bourbon Trail, and Frankfort are where you go to partake in Kentucky's spirit.

PLANNING YOUR TIME

For a satisfying taste of the region, you need to give yourself, at minimum, a four-day weekend. Spend the first day in Bardstown, visiting the distilleries there and in nearby Clermont. Fill any free time with visits to Bardstown's

historic and religious sites. For the next two days, dedicate yourself to enjoying the small towns along the Bourbon Trail—Loretto, Lebanon, and Lawrenceburg. End your trip in Frankfort, where you can fill up on Kentucky history and then finish your bourbon adventure at Buffalo Trace Distillery. Those without an interest in bourbon could still follow this same path, enjoying the scenery and substituting historical and cultural attractions for distilleries. This route—Clermont, Bardstown, Loretto, Lebanon, Lawrenceburg, Frankfort—makes the most sense if you're starting from Louisville. If you're starting from Lexington,

BARDSTOWN

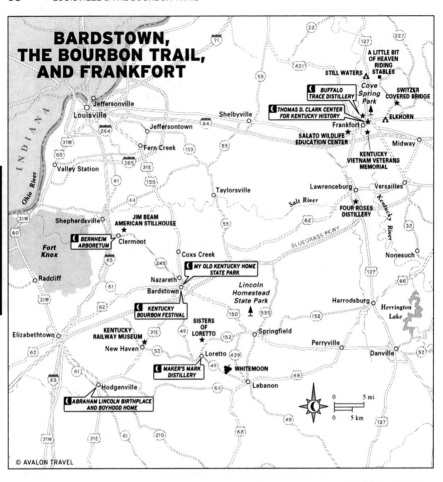

the other popular jumping-off spot for a trip through bourbon country, you can simply flip the route.

To really immerse yourself in this region of Central Kentucky, give yourself a week. You could fit each of the towns in this section into your itinerary with that amount of time, or you could spend a more leisurely time in the towns that interest you the most. Add Hodgenville and Springfield with their many Lincoln attractions to the agenda, and get outdoors either by hiking the Millennium Trail

in Bernheim Arboretum or by paddling with Canoe Kentucky.

If your primary goal is to make it to each of the area's distilleries, you could schedule your trip in two days. You'd have to be meticulous about your itinerary, however, as distilleries offer tours only at set times. You should also note that the distilleries have reduced hours on Sunday, and a few are even closed then. Time of year is also crucial when planning a distillery-based trip. Those with a real interest in the distillation process will want to avoid summer because many of the distilleries go into shutdown during the hottest months. You can still tour the facilities and taste the goods, but you won't see the process in action. Spring and fall are the ideal times to visit this region.

Bardstown

The second oldest town in Kentucky, Bardstown, at first impression, feels a bit like it belongs in the Northeast. Remarkable Federal-style homes line the major thoroughfares, which meet at a traffic circle in which the courthouse sits. Historic markers are chockablock, pointing out the importance of building after building. But take a moment to get to know the town, and you'll realize it's definitively Kentucky. My Old Kentucky Home, the landmark location made into an icon by the state song, is located here, after all. So are major distilleries as well as a craft distillery, the first Catholic cathedral in the West, one of the nation's best Civil War museums, and a slew of restaurants that know how to fry chicken. In Bardstown, you'll find all the components that make this region notable—bourbon sites, religious sites, and historical sites—making it a great starting point for a trip along the Bourbon Trail.

BOURBON SIGHTS
Heaven Hill Distillery
Built of limestone and copper, two elements important to bourbon making, the Bourbon Heritage Center at **Heaven Hill Distillery** (1311 Gilkey Run Rd., 502/337-1000, www.bourbonheritagecenter.com, 10am-5pm Mon.-Sat. year-round, noon-4pm Sun., Mar.-Dec.) is an attractive building loaded with museum-quality exhibits on the history of bourbon that are free to visitors. For those wanting a tour and tasting, you have options: a half-hour Mini-Tour ($4), which includes a guided tour of the Heritage Center and a single tasting; a 1.25-hour Deluxe Tour ($6), which includes a film, a visit to the warehouse, and a tasting of two bourbons; or a 3-hour Behind the Scenes

Tour ($25), which gives you an in-depth look at the entire process behind Heaven Hill's Elijah Craig and Evan Williams bourbons and includes the tasting of two premium bourbons. The tastings, which take place in the barrel-shaped tasting room, are very professionally done, with the guide leading you through a discussion of the taste, smell, and feel of the bourbons. The Behind the Scenes Tour should be booked in advance; other tours can be booked at the center. The last Deluxe Tour departs at 3:40pm Monday-Saturday and at 2:40pm on Sunday.

Barton 1792 Distillery
The **Barton 1792 Distillery** (300 Barton Rd., 502/331-4879, www.1792bourbon.com, 9am-4:30pm Mon.-Fri., 10am-4pm Sat.) is one of a few distilleries that still offer complimentary tours and tastings, so it's a good stop for bourbon fanatics as well as those who aren't sure just how interested they are in distillery touring. The one-hour tours are quite comprehensive, covering everything from the receipt of grains to the fermentation process to bottling and storage, and the guides are both friendly and knowledgeable. When bourbon isn't being distilled, you can still take a tour of the facility and might instead witness the bottling of other liquors. Each tour ends with a tasting of Very Old Barton and 1792 bourbons. Tours are offered on the hour 9am-3pm Monday-Friday and 10am-2pm Saturday.

Willett Distilling Company
On January 18, 2012, the **Willett Distilling Company** (1869 Loretto Rd., 502/348-0899, www.kentuckybourbonwhiskey.com) cooked up its first batch of bourbon using mash bills

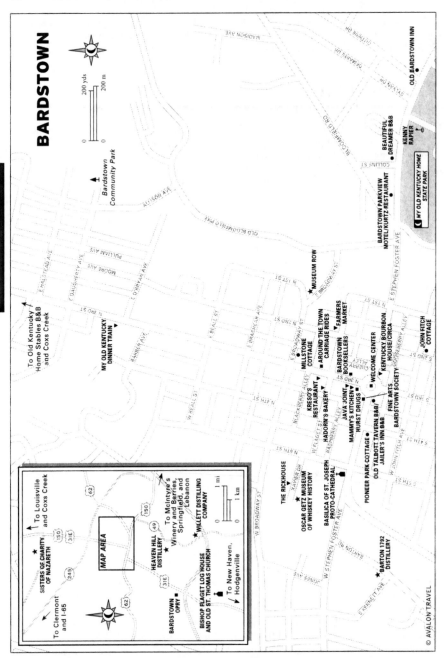

BARDSTOWN

WHAT MAKES BOURBON BOURBON?

Remember in geometry class when you learned that all squares are rectangles, but not all rectangles are squares? Well, bourbon is just like that. All bourbons are whiskeys, but not all whiskeys are bourbons. For a whiskey to be a bourbon whiskey, it must meet a very specific set of criteria.

- It must be made with at least 51 percent corn.
- It must consist of only grain, yeast, and water. No color or flavor can be added.
- It must be aged in brand-new charred white oak barrels for a minimum of two years.
- It must be distilled to no more than 160 proof and barreled at no more than 125 proof.
- It must be bottled at no less than 80 proof.

Additionally, as America's only native spirit, bourbon must be distilled in the United States. Although technically, it can be distilled anywhere in the country, 95 percent of the world's bourbon comes from Kentucky. Two things in particular make Kentucky an ideal place to produce bourbon. The first is the abundance of limestone springs, which produce water that is rich in nutrients but free of flavor. The second is that Kentucky has four very distinct seasons. When bourbon enters the barrel, it is a clear liquid not all that different from moonshine. When it exits the barrel, it is an amber-colored liquid rich with flavors that range from vanilla to spice to caramel to butterscotch. All of bourbon's color and flavor comes from the charred white oak barrel. The charring brings out the sugars in the wood, which the bourbon then absorbs through a process of expanding into the barrel during hot Kentucky summers and then contracting out of it in cold winters. Different varieties of bourbon are produced through both alterations in the recipe and changes in the amount of time the bourbon ages.

Now about the name bourbon. Many residents of and visitors to Kentucky think that Bourbon County was named for the drink, whereas, in fact, the drink was named for the county (which was named for the French royal family). Once an enormous county, Bourbon County was home to the Ohio River port, from which barrels of Kentucky corn whiskey were shipped out to the rest of the country. As the barrels were loaded onto boats, they were stamped with the word "Bourbon" to indicate their port of origin. As Kentucky whiskey gained a following, people began to refer to the liquor as bourbon thanks to the stamp on the barrel. The name stuck, and the best whiskey in the world has been known as bourbon ever since.

Bourbon becomes bourbon while aging in the warehouse.

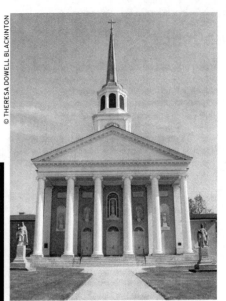

© THERESA DOWELL BLACKINTON

BARDSTOWN

Basilica of St. Joseph Proto-Cathedral

that date back to the original incarnation of this distillery, which produced its first whiskey in 1937. The enormous effort put into restoring the site has paid dividends; this craft distillery, built with wood ceilings and beams and rough-hewn stone walls, is among the most handsome around. Currently, a variety of whiskeys are bottled here, including four boutique bourbons: Kentucky Vintage, Noah's Mill, Pure Kentucky, and Rowan Creek. The very personal and hands-on tours ($7) of the distillery and grounds last between 45 minutes and an hour. Tours are offered 10am-4pm on the hour Monday-Saturday and at 12:30pm, 1:45pm, and 3pm Sunday March-December.

Oscar Getz Museum of Whiskey History

Bourbon and whiskey aficionados can't miss the **Oscar Getz Museum of Whiskey History** (114 N. 5th St., 502/348-2999, www.whiskeymuseum.com, 10am-5pm Mon.-Fri., 10am-4pm Sat., noon-4pm Sun., May-Oct., 10am-4pm Tues.-Sat., noon-4pm Sun., Nov.-Apr., free

admission), which bursts with whiskey-related paraphernalia. You'll find clever advertising art, moonshine stills, Abraham Lincoln's liquor license, antique distilling vessels, and more. The museum, which is a bit tricky to find, is located in Spalding Hall on the St. Joe campus and shares space with the **Bardstown Historical Museum,** a single hall filled with items related to local history.

RELIGIOUS SIGHTS

Basilica of St. Joseph Proto-Cathedral

In 1808, Pope Pius VII created the Diocese of Bardstown, the first Catholic diocese in the West, with jurisdiction over Kentucky, Tennessee, and the entire Northwest Territory. In order to formalize Bardstown's position, Bishop Flaget oversaw the creation of **St. Joseph** (301 W. Stephen Foster Ave., 502/348-3126, www.stjoechurch.com), a majestic cathedral built from bricks baked on the grounds and poplar trees cut from nearby forests and decorated with artwork donated by European royalty. In 1841, when the diocese moved to Louisville, St. Joseph's became a parish church, but as the first cathedral built in the West, it received the name St. Joseph's Proto-Cathedral. In 2001, it was honored with the title of basilica, one of only two in the state. Though you're welcome to explore the basilica on your own, it's best to take advantage of the guided tours, which provide insight into the construction and history of the church as well as the magnificent artwork adorning it. Tours are available on a walk-in basis 9am-5pm Monday-Friday, 9am-3pm Saturday, and 1pm-5pm Sunday, Easter Monday-October. Tours, which may be canceled due to special services, are free, although donations are appreciated.

Bishop Flaget Log House and Old St. Thomas Church

The first permanent residence of the first bishop of the West, the **Bishop Flaget Log House** (870 St. Thomas Ln., 502/348-3717, www.st-thomasparish.org) is considered the oldest structure associated with Catholicism

© THERESA DOWELL BLACKINTON

My Old Kentucky Home

in the Midwest. The restored home is set up to represent the year 1812, when the log building served as a seminary. Old St. Thomas Church, consecrated in 1816 and renovated in 2006, is still the parish home of an active community of Catholics, and visitors are welcome to attend Mass at the church. Tours of the log house are conducted by appointment.

Sisters of Charity of Nazareth

Founded at the Bishop Flaget Log House in 1812 by Mother Catherine Spalding, the **Sisters of Charity of Nazareth** (Nazareth Rd., 502/348-1500, www.scnfamily.org, 9am-4pm Mon.-Sat., 1pm-4pm Sun.) now work in 17 states as well as in Belize, Botswana, India, and Nepal. On a visit to their Nazareth campus, you can watch a short video detailing the good work the sisters do around the world, become acquainted with their heritage in the history room, attend services at St. Vincent, and chat with members of the order. You're also free to explore the manicured grounds, which are graced with many quiet spots ideal for reflection. Additionally, the sisters offer a full schedule of guided spiritual retreats as well as accommodation for private retreatants.

HISTORIC SIGHTS
◖ My Old Kentucky Home State Park

Federal Hill, the home of the distinguished Rowan Family, has become known to generations as My Old Kentucky Home, thanks to Stephen Foster and the song he penned while visiting the home in 1852. The three-story brick house is the centerpiece of **My Old Kentucky Home State Park** (501 E. Stephen Foster Ave., 502/348-3502, http://parks.ky.gov, 9am-4:45pm daily, Mar.-Dec., Wed.-Sun. only, Jan.-Feb.), and costumed tour guides lead visitors through the house, doling out information and anecdotes about family history and the artifacts in the home. An impressive 75 percent of the items in the house, which is decorated in the style of the mid-1800s, actually belonged to the Rowan family. Tours of the house cost $7 for adults, $5 for seniors, and $3.50 for youth 6-12, but visitors to the park are welcome to stroll the grounds, visit the family cemetery, and picnic on the beautifully landscaped lawn free of charge. A designated picnic area with tables, a covered pavilion, and a playground is located on Loretto Road. The park also includes a golf course and campground.

KENTUCKY'S STATE SONG

Every year on Derby Day, as the contenders in America's most prestigious horse race head to the post, the crowd stands for the singing of "My Old Kentucky Home." And without fail, this simple song by Stephen Foster, America's first great composer, brings tears to the eyes of men, women, boys, girls, and jockeys alike. Don't be the only one who doesn't know the words.

My Old Kentucky Home

The sun shines bright on my old
    Kentucky home
'Tis summer, the children are gay
The corn top's ripe and the mead-
    ow's in the bloom
While the birds make music all the
    day
The young folks roll on the little
    cabin floor
All merry, all happy and bright
By 'n' by hard times come a-knock-
    ing at the door
Then my old Kentucky home good-
    night
Weep no more, my lady
Oh, weep no more today
We will sing one song for the old
    Kentucky home
For the old Kentucky home far away

Stephen Foster

Historic Walking Tour

Ask for a copy of the **Historic Walking Tour** brochure at the Welcome Center (1 Court Sq., 502/348-4877), or download it from the tourism website (www.visitbardstown.com); then set out on a 48-stop tour. All sites are within a three-block radius of Court Square. While the brochure gives cursory information on each site, many sites also have informative signs relaying information about architecture and history.

OTHER SIGHTS
Museum Row

Made up of five distinct museums, each of which can be visited individually or as part of a package, **Museum Row** (310 E. Broadway, 502/349-0291, www.civil-war-museum.org, 10am-5pm daily Mar.-Oct., 10am-5pm Fri.-Sun. Nov.-Dec. 15) focuses primarily on history. Tickets ($10 adults, $5 youth 5-15) provide admission to all five museums for two consecutive days.

CIVIL WAR MUSEUM

The most significant of the five museums is the **Civil War Museum**, which has been named the fourth best museum of its type by *North & South*, the official magazine of the Civil War Society. The museum focuses on the action that took place in the Civil War's Western theater (Kentucky, Tennessee, Mississippi, Georgia, and the Carolinas) and portrays the war from both Union and Confederate perspectives. The outer exhibit tells the chronological history of battles while the inner exhibit focuses on more detailed stories, with authentic artifacts illustrating the information. The artifacts on hand are most impressive and include flags, uniforms, weaponry, personal and medical kits, and more, much of which belonged to generals and other high-ranking officers.

WOMEN'S CIVIL WAR MUSEUM

Complementing the Civil War Museum is the **Women's Civil War Museum**, which documents the many ways in which women contributed to the war effort, from acting as nurses, spies, and even soldiers to stepping up to fill roles at home and in the factories.

THE WAR MEMORIAL OF
MID AMERICA MUSEUM

The **War Memorial of Mid America Museum** is the final military-themed attraction on Museum Row. This museum presents artifacts from the Revolutionary War through Desert Storm and tells the story of those who have fought in defense of the United States, with special attention paid to local men and women.

PIONEER VILLAGE

Representing the oldest era of regional history, the **Pioneer Village** strives to authentically re-create a 1790s village. The cabins come from the local area and date back more than 200 years.

WILDLIFE MUSEUM

The final museum in the group, the **Wildlife Museum** focuses on natural history, showcasing professionally stuffed animals of North America in natural-like settings. The preservation is top-notch and the displays are attention-grabbing, especially the one depicting wolves in pursuit of an elk.

McIntyre's Winery and Berries

At **McIntyre's Winery and Berries** (531 McIntyre Ln., 502/507-3264, www.mcintyreswinery.com, 10am-9pm Mon.-Sat., 1pm-9pm Sun.), homegrown blueberries and blackberries are transformed into both sweet and dry fruit wines. Visitors are welcome to stop by for a tour and a tasting.

ENTERTAINMENT
AND EVENTS
Nightlife

Freestanding bars are uncommon in Bardstown and definitely not where the action is. Instead, locals and visitors alike seek out restaurant bars for a drink and evening entertainment. The **Bourbon Bar at Old Talbott Tavern** (107 W. Stephen Foster Ave., 502/348-3494, www.

talbotts.com, 4pm-9pm Mon.-Wed., 4pm-1am Thurs.-Sat., 1pm-8pm Sun.) is a popular gathering place with (loud) live music, and the bar at **The Rickhouse** (112 Xavier Dr., 502/348-2832, 11am-9pm Tues.-Thurs., 11am-10pm Fri.-Sat.) offers a fine selection of bourbons, beers, and wines.

Performing Arts

The Stephen Foster Story (Drama Dr., 502/348-5971, www.stephenfoster.com) is Bardstown's signature performance, drawing big crowds every summer with its song-and-dance-filled story of America's first great composer. Unless it rains, the evening performances take place at the large outdoor theater on the grounds of My Old Kentucky Home State Park. In addition to putting on the classic *Stephen Foster Story*, the Stephen Foster Productions company rounds out the schedule with other musical performances. For instance, the 2013 schedule featured *Shrek the Musical*. The season runs mid-June-mid-August, and tickets cost $19-24 for adults and $11-13 for youth 6-12.

Live Music

The **Live at the Park Concert Series** (502/348-5971, www.stephenfoster.com) brings popular (but sometimes dated) musicians to town to perform onstage at My Old Kentucky Home State Park. The 2013 concerts featured John Michael Montgomery, Jana Kramer, The Monarchs, The Devonshires, and Beatles and CCR tribute bands. Tickets range $15-25; those interested in multiple shows should consider purchasing season tickets, which are good for the concerts as well as the Stephen Foster Story productions.

Music lovers will also want to avail themselves of the free **Summer Band Concerts,** which are held 7pm-9pm every Friday Memorial Day-Labor Day in the **Bardstown Community Park** (E. Halstead Ave., www.cityofbardstown.org). Bands and genres change every week, so pack a picnic and make it a recurring date.

The Bardstown Opry (426 Sutherland Rd.,

859/336-9839, www.musicmansoundstage. com, $10 adults, $6 youth 6-12) caters to bluegrass fans with shows every Friday night. Doors open at 6pm, with music from 7:30pm to 10pm.

Festivals and Events
(KENTUCKY BOURBON FESTIVAL
For six days in mid-September, the Bourbon Capital of the World hosts the **Kentucky Bourbon Festival** (800/638-4877, www.ky-bourbonfestival.com), an absolute must for lovers of America's native spirit. Highlights of the festival include the Great Kentucky Bourbon Tasting and Gala and the Kentucky Bourbon All-Star Sampler. Each of these events allows participants to meet with master distillers and taste the best bourbons being made. Although much of the schedule is filled with events directly related to bourbon (demonstrations, seminars, tastings, and more), you'll also find golf tournaments, fun runs, art festivals, concerts, and other types of entertainment to keep you satisfied between sips.

BARDSTOWN ARTS, CRAFTS & ANTIQUES FAIR
Nearly 200 artists and craftspeople descend on Bardstown on the second weekend of October for the **Bardstown Arts, Crafts & Antiques Fair** (www.visitbardstown.com), held on the streets of downtown. Shop for jewelry, pottery, woodwork, photography, prints, and more while enjoying music and local food.

SHOPPING
North Third Street is lined with shops selling gifts, apparel, and local souvenirs, so window shop as you walk, popping in whenever something catches your eye. At **Bardstown Booksellers** (129 N. 3rd St., 502/348-1256, 9am-6pm Mon.-Thurs., 9am-7pm Fri.-Sat., 11am-4pm Sun.), books about Kentucky fill the most prominent shelves, so it's a great place to shop if you're looking for a cookbook of traditional recipes or a coffee table book of beautiful photos. The store also stocks locally made crafts, jewelry, and food, including a mouthwatering selection of truffles, as well as popular and antiquarian books.

Old-fashioned **Hurst Drugs** (102 N. 3rd St., 502/348-9261, 8am-6pm Mon.-Sat.) stocks a broad selection of Kentucky souvenirs, including Derby glasses, U of L and UK themed gifts, pottery, and Kentucky Proud food products. You're also welcome to have a seat at one of the red stools at the counter and enjoy a shake, malt, float, or soda.

At the gallery of the **Fine Arts Bardstown Society** (90 Court Sq., 502/348-0044, www.fineartsbardstown.com, 10am-6pm Tues.-Sat., noon-6pm Sun.), you'll find photography, pottery, sculpture, jewelry, and all sorts of other artwork produced by the society's members.

SPORTS AND RECREATION
Golf
The **Kenny Rapier Golf Course** (668 Loretto Rd., 502/349-6542, http://parks.ky.gov, Apr.-Oct.), which is part of My Old Kentucky Home State Park, is an 18-hole, par-71 course. It was awarded four stars by *Golf Digest* in 2009 after a redesign that updated the original 1928 course to a more modern style.

ACCOMMODATIONS
$50-100
Bardstown Parkview Motel (418 E. Stephen Foster Ave., 502/348-5983, www.bardstown-parkview.com, $60-100) doesn't claim to offer all the amenities of new hotels, but instead preserves the style that made motels popular in the first place. Service at this family-owned place is friendly, the grounds are nicely manicured, and a courtyard area with pool is popular with families. Though dated, rooms and suites (which have desks and cooktops) are clean and come with Internet connections. The location directly across the street from My Old Kentucky Home can't be beat. Breakfast isn't worth getting up for.

The 33 units at **Old Bardstown Inn** (510 E. Stephen Foster Ave., 502/349-0776, www.angelfire.com/ky3/oldbardstowninn, $55) offer standard motel amenities with clean rooms, each with two queen beds, wireless Internet access, and refrigerators. A continental breakfast is served in the lobby, and a pool provides a welcome escape on hot summer days. Leave your car in the lot and just cross the street to visit My Old Kentucky Home or play a round of golf.

The five rooms at **Old Talbott Tavern Bed and Breakfast** (107 W. Stephen Foster Ave., 502/348-3494, www.talbotts.com, $69-109) are named for famous Tavern guests: Abraham Lincoln, Generals Clark and Patton, Anton Heinrich, Daniel Boone, and Washington Irving. All rooms are furnished with period antiques, such as claw-foot tubs and canopy beds, but contain modern (but worn) amenities like private baths, refrigerators, and TVs. Beware that the rooms can be very noisy due to both street traffic and the music played in the bar below. Breakfast is disappointing, especially considering the B&B is part of a restaurant.

$100-150

At the **Jailer's Inn Bed and Breakfast** (111 W. Stephen Foster Ave., 502/348-5551, www.jailersinn.com, $110-155), you don't have to break any laws to spend the night in the slammer. While the back jail remains preserved, the front jail has been renovated to contain six guest rooms. Five feel like typical B&B rooms, while one room, decorated in black and white and with the original bunks, maintains the aura of a jail cell. Plenty of ghost stories surround the jail, so a stay here might not be for the faint of heart. A family suite ($235) with one king bed, one queen bed, and a living area is also available.

Book a room at **Old Kentucky Home Stables Bed and Breakfast** (115 Samuels Rd., Cox's Creek, 502/294-0474, $115), located 10 minutes from downtown Bardstown, and you'll be spending the night at America's oldest continuously operating saddlebred horse farm. The pre-Civil War home, with original plank floors and double-sided brick fireplace, offers large rooms with all the modern amenities, including whirlpool tubs and cable TV. Views stretch far and wide over rural countryside, and are only occasionally interrupted by a peacock strutting past, feathers spread. Owner Frankie is a history and horse buff and can ply you with trivia or spin a good story. You can also arrange riding lessons with him, though be aware that the saddlebreds he breeds, trains, and shows are big, powerful animals, not ponies.

$150-200

Named for one of Stephen Foster's songs, ◖ **Beautiful Dreamer Bed and Breakfast** (440 E. Stephen Foster Ave., 502/348-4004, www.bdreamerbb.com, $159-189) sits on property that was once part of My Old Kentucky Home. Now a street divides it from this landmark, but you can still enjoy a view of the park from the second-floor veranda. The four spacious bedrooms have large bathrooms, flat-screen TVs, reclining chairs, and big beds. Decor is crisp and classic, and the walls are painted in shades of rich wine, forest green, and Kentucky blue. Breakfast is served family style, and drinks and snacks, along with games and DVDs, are available on the second-floor landing. If you have questions about the Stephen Foster Story, which you can walk to from the B&B, just ask host Lynell. She's seen the show more than 200 times!

The **Colonel's Cottage Inns** (502/507-8338, www.colonelscottageinns.com) are three meticulously restored 19th-century cottages, each of which is available to be rented by those looking for a private retreat along the Bourbon Trail. **Millstone Cottage** (107 E. Broadway, $169) has two bedrooms, one with a queen bed and the other with two single beds, and a bathroom with whirlpool tub for two and shower. **Pioneer Park Cottage** (114 S. Fourth St., $189) also has two bedrooms, one with a queen bed and the other with two single beds, but it has two bathrooms, one with a whirlpool tub and one with a shower. **John Fitch Cottage** (211 E. John Fitch, $129) has one queen bedroom and a bathroom with both whirlpool tub and shower. All have kitchens, living areas, and outdoor space. The cottages are tidied up daily and breakfast is left in the kitchen, but otherwise guests are left in privacy.

Campgrounds

My Old Kentucky Home State Park hosts a **campground** (Loretto Rd., 502/348-3502, http://parks.ky.gov, Apr.-Oct., $23), which has 39 improved sites for RVs and a separate grassy area for tent campers. Showers and restrooms are located in a central building.

FOOD

My Old Kentucky Dinner Train

Take your dinner in a vintage 1940s dinner car while enjoying a ride through the countryside on **My Old Kentucky Dinner Train** (N. 3rd St., 502/348-7300, www.rjcorman.com, dinner trip $84.95 adult, $54.95 youth 5-12, lunch trip $69.95 adult, $44.95 youth 5-12). During the 2.5-hour trip, a four-course dinner or three-course lunch is served, with travelers choosing from a small selection of options for their salad, entrée, and dessert. The train runs year-round, although there are more departures during summer months. Visit the website to view the schedule and make reservations.

Kentucky Bourbon House

At the ◖ **Kentucky Bourbon House** (107 E. Stephen Foster Ave., 502/507-8338, www.chapezehouse.com), Colonel Michael and Margaret Sue Masters bring together the best of bourbon and Southern cooking for a memorable lunch or dinner experience. Lunch is served as part of **Kentucky Bourbon University** ($99), where participants learn about bourbon history, production, and etiquette and how to drink and serve bourbon. The class features 10 premium Kentucky bourbons, two rye whiskies, one Tennessee whiskey, and one white dog, and it ends with a classic lunch of burgoo, country ham, Benedictine, potato salad, and bread pudding. Dinners ($29.95) are intimate events limited to 20 guests. They begin at 6:30 with bourbon and cocktails and then proceed into a dinner of bourbon-marinated pork chops accompanied by a bevy of fresh sides and finished with dessert. Reservations are required for both lunch and dinner, which are unique experiences akin to dining with gracious Southern friends in their historic home.

Farmers Market

Pick up crisp veggies, juicy fruits, and other farm-fresh products at the **Farmers Market** (N. 2nd and E. Flaget Sts., 7:30am-12:30pm Tues., Fri., and Sat., May-Oct.), held three times a week in a permanent building in downtown Bardstown.

Cafés and Bakeries

If you've got a hankering for a pastry or other baked goodie, head to **Hadorn's Bakery** (118 W. Flaget St., 502/348-4407, 7am-1pm Tues.-Sat., $0.95-3.95), where treats are turned out fresh each day.

Java Joint (126 N. 3rd St., 502/350-0883, 7:30am-5:30pm Mon.-Sat., $5.50-6.75) keeps Bardstown fueled with coffee and specialty drinks all day long, and during the lunch stretch offers a selection of soups, salads, and sandwiches. In addition to the common chicken and egg salad, Java Joint also serves muffulettas, Cubans, and a roasted pepper pimento cheese.

Contemporary American

Located right on Bardstown's main circle in a yellow-painted stone house dating to around 1780, ◖ **Circa** (103 E. Stephen Foster Ave., 502/348-5409, www.restaurant-circa.com, lunch 11am-2pm Tues.-Fri., dinner 5pm-9pm Tues.-Sat., $21-30) serves a small menu of upscale contemporary Southern food at reclaimed poplar tables spread throughout various rooms of the house. Dinner choices might include lamb pot pie or coq au vin. The lunch menu ($7-10) ranges from fish tacos to chicken crepes to mac and cheese with turkey, bacon, and tomato. Expect excellent service and a special-occasion feel. Reservations are recommended.

Classic American

Hidden away in the basement under the Oscar Getz Museum, **The Rickhouse** (Xavier Dr., 502/348-2832, http://market8media.com/therickhouse, 11am-9pm Tues.-Thurs., 11am-10pm Fri.-Sat., $14-27) serves well-prepared classic American dishes while playing to a bourbon theme. Steaks are a signature item, but other favorites include a barbecue bourbon chicken, a porterhouse pork chop, and a Hot Brown. Try the Brussels sprouts as a side... seriously.

If you want to know what good fried chicken tastes like, get a table at **Kurtz Restaurant** (418 E. Stephen Foster Ave., 502/348-8964, www.bardstownparkview.com, 11am-9pm Tues.-Sat., noon-8pm Sun., $13.95-18.95), where it's served piping hot and without a hint of grease though it's cooked the way grandma used to do it—in a skillet full of lard. You also don't want to miss the fried cornbread, enormous pieces of meringue pie, or the biscuit pudding with bourbon raisin sauce. Kurtz has been serving fried chicken and other Southern favorites since 1937, and when you step into the home-turned-restaurant, you'll be treated like one of the family. The atmosphere is cozy with dining tables spread through the rooms of the house.

Those who like their meals served with a side of history will appreciate the **Old Talbott Tavern** (107 W. Stephen Foster Ave., 502/348-3494, www.talbotts.com, 11am-9pm Mon.-Thurs., 11am-10pm Fri.-Sat., 11am-7pm Sun., $14.95-29.95), which dates back to 1779 and maintains much of its original architecture. George Rogers Clark used the tavern as his base during the Revolutionary War, and other famous figures who have passed through the doors include Andrew Jackson, Abraham Lincoln, John James Audubon, and General George Patton. Though portions of fried chicken, catfish, pork chops, and country ham are large, flavors need to be kicked up a notch. Unlike the atmosphere, the food is rather bland.

Mammy's Kitchen (114 N. Third St., 502/350-1097, 6:30am-8pm Mon.-Tues., 6:30am-9pm Wed.-Fri., 8am-2pm Sun.) is your destination if you're after no-fuss but tasty home cooking along the lines of chicken fried chicken, open-faced roast beef sandwiches, and meatloaf. Breakfast is served until 11am, and there's always pie, with the meringue on the chocolate, coconut, and butterscotch piled high. It's a small place that's nearly always busy, but service is speedy, so your wait shouldn't be too long.

European

Kreso's Restaurant (218 N. 3rd St., 502/348-9594, www.kresosrestaurant.com, lunch 11am-3pm Mon.-Fri., dinner 5pm-11pm Mon.-Fri., 11am-11pm Sat., noon-10pm Sun., $9.95-26) exudes charm thanks to the fact that it's located in an old theater. Run by a Bosnian family, the menu offers old-world favorites like schnitzel and goulash, as well as an excellent selection of steaks and seafood (and not the fried kind most popular in these parts). Start any meal with the Bosnian salad, a mix of leaf lettuce, tomato, cucumber, hard-boiled egg, red onion, and feta cheese. The lunch menu ($6.95-9.95) includes lighter versions of popular dinner entrées as well as salads and sandwiches. Service can be hit-or-miss.

INFORMATION AND SERVICES

Gather all the information you can handle at Bardstown's **Welcome Center** (1 Court Sq., 502/348-4877, www.visitbardstown.com), located in the courthouse building smack in the middle of the main traffic circle. Bardstown's main **post office** (205 W. Stephen Foster Ave.) is located just down the street.

GETTING THERE

Bardstown is about 40 miles (45 minutes) south of Louisville. Take I-65 South to KY 245 South (Exit 112). After 15 miles, turn right on 3rd Street, which leads straight to the center of town. For a more scenic drive, take U.S. 31E (Bardstown Road) all the way from Louisville to Bardstown. From Frankfort (55 miles; one hour) or Lexington (60 miles; one hour), going eastbound on Blue Grass Parkway (KY 9002) will connect you to U.S. 31.

Bardstown lies 165 miles (2.25 hours) northeast of Nashville via northbound I-65 to the Blue Grass Parkway (Exit 93) to U.S. 31. Bardstown is 302 miles (4.5 hours) from St. Louis, 154 miles (2.5 hours) from Indianapolis,

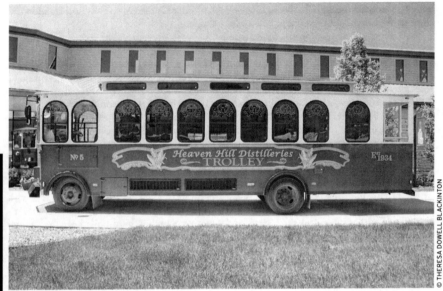

© THERESA DOWELL BLACKINTON

Heaven Hill Distilleries Trolley

and 140 miles (2.25 hours) from Cincinnati. Coming from any of these three cities, you'll first travel to Louisville, and then follow the directions from there.

GETTING AROUND
Trolley Tours
See Bardstown from the windows of the **Heaven Hill Distilleries Trolley** (www.bourbonheritagecenter.com) on a narrated half-hour tour. The handsome vintage trolley leaves from

the distillery and circles past the town's main attractions. The tours run at 10am and 1pm.

Carriage Tours
Take in historic Bardstown at a relaxed pace with **Around the Town Carriage Rides** (223 N. 3rd St., 502/249-0889, 9am-10pm daily). Horse-drawn carriages, buggies, and stagecoaches provide the most stylish rides in town. A 30-minute narrated tour for two people costs $40.

Vicinity of Bardstown

A few small towns surround Bardstown to the south and east and are worth a visit for their religious and historical sites. Railway enthusiasts and those moved by the writings of Thomas Merton will want to add New Haven to their itinerary, while Lincoln fans shouldn't miss Hodgenville, the president's hometown, and Springfield, his ancestral home.

NEW HAVEN
Abbey of Gethsemani
Since 1848, Trappist monks have called the **Abbey of Gethsemani** (3642 Monks Rd., Trappist, 502/549-3117, www.monks.org) home, dedicating the time they spend at this beautiful sanctuary to formal prayers and the manual labor that provides their livelihood.

© THERESA DOWELL BLACKINTON

Abbey of Gethsemani

10am-4pm Tues.-Sat., noon-4pm Sun., $5 adults, $2 youth 2-12) and a ride on one of their trains. The trains cover 22 miles of countryside on a 90-minute ride, with a brief layover at the turnaround point allowing a chance to grab a snack or drink. Those who have dreamed of engineering a train can opt to ride in the locomotive ($50 adults, $25 youth 7-12). Special events are held throughout the year. Among the most popular are the Great Train Robbery weekends, Mystery Theatre nights, and holiday-themed trips. If you have kids, you won't want to miss Thomas the Tank Engine's visit, which occurs each summer and draws huge crowds. Train rides are offered at 2pm on Saturday and Sunday March-May and mid-August-mid-December; and at 11am and 2pm on Saturday, 2pm on Sunday, and 1pm on Tuesday and Friday mid-June-mid-August. Train fares ($17 adults, $12 youth 2-12 on diesel trains; $2 more on steam trains) include admission to the museum, which features rail artifacts, and the model train center, which hosts detailed displays that can be activated by visitors.

Getting There and Around

New Haven is located 13.5 miles (18 minutes) south of Bardstown and can be reached via southbound U.S. 31E. To reach the Abbey of Gethsemani, you don't have to travel all the way into New Haven. Instead, after eight miles on U.S. 31E, turn left onto Monks Road.

HODGENVILLE

Though Illinois claims to be the Land of Lincoln, America's 16th president was a Kentuckian by birth and spent the first seven years of his life in the Bluegrass State. More specifically, young Abe grew up in the area that came to be known as Hodgenville, but was a frontier town at the time. The early years of his life, a time of struggle (although his family would have been considered middle class), certainly helped shape the man who would become president. In fact, in an autobiography he wrote for his 1860 campaign, Lincoln noted that his earliest memories revolved around his boyhood home on Knobs Creek. Today's

Gethsemani is widely known thanks to Thomas Merton, a Trappist monk at the abbey who wrote multiple books, including his famous autobiography *The Seven Storey Mountain,* and attracted admirers with his interest in interfaith understanding. Visitors to the abbey are greeted in the Welcome Center (9am-5pm Mon.-Sat.) with a video that explains the monastic life, and are also invited to join the monks at prayers or Mass. In the longstanding tradition of monks offering hospitality, people interested in prayer and reflection are welcome to reserve a stay at the **abbey** (502/549-4133, by donation). Directed retreats are also available through the **Merton Institute Retreat Center at Bethany Spring** (502/549-8277, www.bethanyspring.org). Visitors to the Abbey of Gethsemani should remember that it is a place of silent prayer.

Kentucky Railway Museum

Chug back in time with a visit to the **Kentucky Railway Museum** (136 S. Main St., New Haven, 502/549-5470, www.kyrail.org,

Memorial Building at Abraham Lincoln Birthplace

Hodgenville celebrates this connection with a number of Lincoln-related sites.

Abraham Lincoln Birthplace and Boyhood Home

Part of the National Park Service, the **Abraham Lincoln Birthplace** (2995 Lincoln Farm Rd., 270/358-3137, www.nps.gov/abli, 8am-4:45pm daily, Sept.-May, 8am-6:45pm daily, June-Aug., free) and **Boyhood Home** (7 miles north on U.S. 31E) preserve a sense of how the Lincoln family lived in Kentucky. Begin your visit at the Birthplace Visitors Center, where you can view a 15-minute film about Lincoln's childhood and check out the Lincoln family bible and other artifacts. The site's main attraction is the Memorial Building, a marble and granite structure that houses a cabin symbolic of that in which Lincoln was born. Fifty-six steps, one for each year of Lincoln's life, lead up to the memorial and past the Sinking Spring, for which the family farm was named. (The Pathway of a President trail provides wheelchair access to the memorial.) A 0.7-mile interpretive hiking trail is open to those who want to stretch their legs and learn a bit about what the Lincoln homestead would have been like. After visiting the Birthplace, continue on to Lincoln's Boyhood Home, where he lived from 1811 to 1816. Poke your head in the family cabin of Lincoln's friend Austin Gollaher, wander down to the creek where Lincoln almost drowned in a flash flood, and examine a garden planted with crops the Lincolns likely grew.

Lincoln Museum

At the **Lincoln Museum** (66 Lincoln Square, 270/358-3163, www.lincolnmuseum-ky.org, 8:30am-4:30pm Mon.-Sat., 12:30pm-4:30pm Sun., $3 adults, $2.50 seniors, $1.50 youth 5-12), 12 life-size dioramas depict important events in the life of the 16th president—from his cabin years in Kentucky to his assassination at Ford's Theatre. The well-done dioramas make history accessible to children and those with only a cursory interest in the subject, while accompanying photos, newspaper articles, letters, and descriptive panels cater to those seeking more in-depth information. A second floor contains Lincoln artwork as well as Civil War artifacts, including items unearthed from battlefield digs.

Lincoln Square Statues

In the center of Hodgenville, two statues of Abraham Lincoln sit facing each other. Dedicated in 1909, Adolph Weinman's Abraham Lincoln Statue depicts the Kentuckian seated and looking as he did when he was president. Directly across from this classic statue you'll find the more whimsical Boy Lincoln Statue, added to the square in 2008. This statue shows young Abe, accompanied by a dog and a fishing pole, leaning against a tree stump and reading from a Webster's spelling book.

Entertainment

For a toe-tapping good time that apparently even the President would have loved, make plans to attend the **Lincoln Jamboree** (2579 Lincoln Farm Rd., 270/358-3545, www.lincolnjamboree.com, 7:30pm-10:30pm Sat., $8.50), an old-fashioned country music show that's been going strong for more than 50 years. Come early to enjoy free music on the patio (6pm).

Events

To honor the city's, as well as the state's, greatest resident, Hodgenville celebrates **Lincoln Days** (270/358-8710, www.lincolndays.org) annually in late September or early October. The weekend festival includes an oratory contest, Mary Todd and Abraham Lincoln lookalike contests, and pioneer games, as well as art and car shows, a parade, a fun run, and live music.

Food

Laha's Red Castle (21 Lincoln Square, 270/358-9201, 9am-4pm Mon.-Tues. and Thurs.-Sat., 9am-1:30pm Wed., $1.95-4.95) has been keeping Hodgenville in hamburgers for more than 65 years. Follow the smell of fried onions to the tiny corner diner, where

you'll most likely have to wait for a stool at the counter to open up before you can place your order for a fresh-made hamburger and an ice-cold bottled Coke.

Follow up your lunch with a treat from **The Sweet Shoppe** (100 S. Lincoln Blvd., 270/358-0424, www.sweetshoppefudge.com, 11am-6pm Mon.-Sat.), which offers 35 flavors of fudge, along with ice cream and other desserts. A half-pound of fudge sells for $4.99.

Information and Services

The **LaRue County Visitors Center** (60 Lincoln Sq., 270/358-3411, www.laruecountychamber.org, 9am-4pm Mon.-Fri.) can set you up with all the information you need on Hodgenville's attractions as well as other regional sites of interest.

Getting There

Hodgenville is located 25 miles (30 minutes) southwest of Bardstown via southbound U.S. 31E. Hodgenville can also be reached by exiting I-65 at southbound KY 61 (Exit 91), which will lead you right to the center of town.

SPRINGFIELD

Complementing Hodgenville is the town of Springfield, which is where President Lincoln's pioneer grandparents settled and where both of his parents were born and raised.

Lincoln Homestead State Park

Abraham Lincoln's ancestors entered Kentucky in the late 1700s via the Wilderness Road, establishing a homestead in the area that is now Springfield. **Lincoln Homestead State Park** (5079 Lincoln Park Rd., 859/336-7461, http://parks.ky.gov) is home to three structures that preserve the history of the Lincoln family. The Lincoln Cabin is a replica of the log house in which Abraham Lincoln's grandmother lived and raised five children, including President Lincoln's father, Thomas. A second log house at the park, which is a bit fancier with a second floor and glass windows, was the home of President Lincoln's mother, Nancy Hanks. This original cabin was moved to the park from

© THERESA DOWELL BLACKINTON

BARDSTOWN

President Lincoln's mother's house at Lincoln Homestead State Park

about a mile away. A third building, a stately white home that belonged to President Lincoln's favorite uncle, Mordecai Lincoln, is also in the park, having been moved from across the street. Tours of the cabins along with a blacksmith's shop cost $2 for adults and $1.50 for youth, and are offered 10:30am-5:30pm daily, May-September, and on weekends in October. The grounds, which are complete with signage relaying the history of the buildings and area, are free and open year-round.

Opposite the road from the homes is an 18-hole golf course, allowing you to play a round on the rolling hills where the Lincolns once lived.

Mt. Zion Covered Bridge

At 246 feet long, the **Mt. Zion Covered Bridge** (KY 458), which crosses the Beech Fork River, is one of the longest remaining multispan bridges in Kentucky. Built in 1871, Mt. Zion Covered Bridge is the only one of Washington County's seven covered bridges to remain standing, although it is no longer in use.

Accommodations

🄲 **Maple Hill Manor** (2941 Perryville Rd., 859/336-3075, www.maplehillmanor.com, $139-199) deserves the many raves and honors it has received, and it's worth going a bit out of your way to stay here. Set on a 15-acre working alpaca and llama farm and surrounded by horse, tobacco, and cattle farms, this wonderfully preserved antebellum home has seven lovely guest rooms, each with private bath. The large, light-filled rooms are luxurious with plush bedding, towels, and robes, along with high-end bath products, fireplaces, TVs, and Internet access. Homemade desserts and beverages are offered each evening in the parlor, and a candlelight breakfast is served on fine china in the formal dining room each morning. Guests are invited to tour the grounds, which are complete with flower gardens, fish ponds, and an orchard from which you can pick fresh fruit in season. Although convenient to Springfield attractions and the Bourbon Trail, Maple Hill Manor is also the perfect place to go and do nothing but relax. Football fans take note: Maple Hill Manor was the childhood home of Super Bowl MVP and Giants quarterback Phil Simms.

Food

Signature dishes at **Mordecai's on Main** (105 W. Main St., 859/336-3500, www.mordecaisonmain.com, 11am-midnight Tues.-Sat., 10am-2pm Sun., $6.99-18.49) include honey bourbon salmon, chicken in a mushroom bourbon cream sauce, New York strip marinated in bourbon, and bourbon-marinated pork chops, making it a perfect place for Bourbon Trail visitors to dine. If you've already had enough bourbon, the menu also offers burgers, sandwiches, and entrées prepared in other tasty ways. Located in a downtown building, Mordecai's is decorated with historic photos and offers a variety of seating options, including patio seating in the summer. Good food and good service make this Springfield's best dining option. The Friday and Saturday buffet is extremely popular, offering a selection of entrées as well as soup and salad.

THE BOURBON CHASE

Although most people choose to cover the Bourbon Trail in an automobile, some believe the best way to take in the landscape of this part of Kentucky is on foot—hence, the reason the annual **Bourbon Chase** (www.bourbonchase.com), a 200-mile relay race along the Bourbon Trail, sells out every year months before its October start date.

Teams of 6 or 12 members begin the race at Jim Beam Distillery in Clermont, with teams taking off every 15 minutes during the first day. Each runner covers 3-9 miles before being replaced by a teammate. The course moves from Clermont to Bardstown, then passes through Loretto, Lebanon, Springfield, Perryville, Stanford, Danville, Harrodsburg, Lawrenceburg, Versailles, Frankfort, and Midway before ending in Lexington, where a huge party awaits participants. The race can take up to 35 hours, with runners pounding the pavement both day and night. Towns along the way are set up to support and celebrate the teams regardless of what hour the runners and their teammates pass through.

Autumn is a beautiful time of year to visit the Bourbon Trail region of Kentucky, so whether you're interested in participating in the race or just cheering on the runners, put the Bourbon Chase on your calendar.

Information and Services

The **Springfield Tourism Commission** (127 W. Main St., 859/336-5440, www.seespringfieldky.com, 9am-5pm Mon.-Fri.) has an office in the restored Opera House. After you gather any information you need, take a few minutes for an informal tour of the building, which was built around 1900 and renovated in 2004.

Getting There and Around

Springfield is 17 miles (25 minutes) east of Bardstown on U.S. 150. Located right past the intersection of U.S. 150 and KY 55, Springfield is on the route between Bardstown and Lebanon and thus easy to add to any Bourbon Trail itinerary.

The Bourbon Trail and Nearby Towns

In 1999, the Kentucky Distillers Association decided to turn one of the state's most distinct industries into what is now one of its biggest tourist attractions, creating an official Bourbon Trail. This official trail, which highlights seven distilleries, serves as a great starting point for those seeking to get a taste of Kentucky, both literally and figuratively. However, bourbon fanatics will want to go beyond the trail to visit additional major distilleries as well as the craft distilleries that have opened in recent years, feeding off the bourbon craze. Not all of Kentucky's bourbon sites are located in this region, but the area is definitely the heart of bourbon country. It's also home to small towns and rolling countryside, where the Kentucky spirit is distilled day in and day out.

CLERMONT

For those starting the trail from Louisville, Clermont will be your first stop. Not actually a city or even a town, Clermont is just a small stretch of road that happens to be home to the world's largest bourbon distillery. Most bourbon tourists group Clermont in with Bardstown, which is just a bit further down the road.

Jim Beam American Stillhouse

In an idyllic setting, **Jim Beam American**

Stillhouse (526 Happy Hollow Rd., 502/543-9877, www.americanstillhouse.com, 9am-5:30pm Mon.-Sat., noon-4:30pm Sun. Mar.-Dec.) is definitely worth a visit since the distillery's upgrade and expansion in 2012. Guided tours ($10) begin at the natural limestone water well and don't end until you've seen every part of the process, from mashing to distilling, barreling, storing, and bottling. Tours end with your choice of two tastings from a selection of 15 options. The 1.25-hour tours, which are very hands-on and allow you to participate in the distilling process, are offered on the half-hour 9:30am-3:30pm Monday-Saturday and 12:30pm-3pm Sunday. Twice a month, a six-hour bourbon experience ($199) that includes a meeting with the master distiller, a meal, and a commemorative bottle of bourbon are offered, giving the true connoisseur an insider's experience. Reservations are highly recommended.

Four Roses Warehouses

Although their distillery is located in Lawrenceburg, **Four Roses** maintains their bottling facilities and warehouse off-site (624 Lotus Rd., Cox's Creek, 502/543-2664, http://fourrosesbourbon.com). Unique among bourbon distilleries, Four Roses uses single-story warehouses to age their bourbon, believing this helps minimize temperature fluctuations and creates a more consistent taste. True bourbon aficionados may want to arrange a tour of the facilities, available by reservation only.

◖ Bernheim Arboretum

Grateful for his success in the whiskey business, Isaac W. Bernheim chose to give back to the state of Kentucky by purchasing 14,000 acres for use as an arboretum. Designed by the Olmsted landscape firm, **Bernheim Arboretum and Research Center** (2499 Old State Hwy. 245, 502/955-8512, www.bernheim.org, 7am-sunset daily, free weekdays, $5 per car weekends and holidays) opened to the public in 1950 and has since become an oasis for people all around the region. Begin your

visit at the LEED Platinum Certified Visitors Center, a magnificent "green" building where you can pick up maps, learn about the arboretum, browse the gift shop, or enjoy a snack or light lunch at the café. The arboretum offers plenty of activities. Those seeking more passive recreation opportunities can picnic, view wildlife, and wander around the arboretum's many gardens and collections, including an open prairie habitat and the largest holly collection in North America. If you're after something more active, take advantage of the arboretum's 35 miles of hiking trails, 3.7-mile bike trail, roadside bike lanes, and the fishing areas at Lake Nevin. Be sure to check out the Canopy Tree Walk, a boardwalk that puts you 75 feet over the forest floor and offers splendid views year-round, though autumn is especially breathtaking. Hikers will find the 13.75-mile Millennium Trail through the knobs of Kentucky to be one of the region's best trails. Bernheim offers a robust schedule of events that includes moonlight hikes, ECO Kids activities, art classes, and seasonal festivities. Check their website for a full listing.

Accommodations and Food

Just north of Bernheim and Jim Beam, you'll find a strip of fast-food restaurants as well as a chain hotel or two. There's no real reason to stay overnight in the area, and with Clermont located between Bardstown and Louisville, you have plenty of options in either direction. Your best bet for lunch is to bring a picnic and enjoy it on the grounds of Bernheim or check out the tasty sandwiches at their café.

Getting There

Clermont is about 15 miles (20 minutes) northwest of Bardstown. From the center of Bardstown, take Third Street to northbound KY 245, where you'll turn left and then travel about 13.5 miles to reach Clermont's attractions.

Clermont is about 27 miles (30 minutes) south of downtown Louisville. To get to Clermont, simply follow southbound I-65 to the KY 245 exit (Exit 112). Turn left onto KY

245, and you'll find Bernheim on your right and Jim Beam just past it on your left.

LORETTO

After you check out the distilleries in Clermont and Bardstown, the next stop on your west-to-east tour of Kentucky's bourbon distilleries is Loretto. Best described as a hamlet, Loretto, with a population of about 600, probably wouldn't make the map if it weren't for the iconic Maker's Mark distillery being located here.

◖ Maker's Mark Distillery

Set on a village-like campus, **Maker's Mark Distillery** (3350 Burks Spring Rd., 270/865-2099, www.makersmark.com) wins the award for most picturesque distillery. The buildings are uniformly dark brown, tan, and red—the trademark colors of Maker's Mark—with cut-out bourbon bottles on every window shutter. The tour starts in a home museum decorated to the 1950 period when the Samuels family began Maker's Mark. It then takes in the spotless distillery, where bourbon is still brewed in

© THERESA DOWELL BLACKINTON

Maker's Mark Distillery

wooden vats; the bottling line, where the bottles are dipped in their famous red wax; and the warehouse, where barrels are still rotated during their six-year aging process. The finale is a well-conducted tasting of bourbon at four different stages, complemented with a bourbon ball. Tours ($9) are offered once an hour on the half-hour 9:30am-3:30pm Monday-Saturday year-round and 11:30am-3:30pm Sunday, March-December.

Sisters of Loretto

Founded on the Kentucky frontier in 1812, the **Sisters of Loretto** (515 Nerinx Rd., 270/865-7096, www.lorettocommunity.org) moved to their current campus in 1824. Visitors are welcome on the campus, a place of mesmerizing beauty that, in addition to preserving vast wild spaces, also supports a working farm and many historical buildings. Don't miss the Rhodes Hall Art Gallery, where the amazing sculptures of Sister Jeanne Dueber are displayed. You'll also want to stroll the walking paths and visit the cemetery and AIDS garden. A Heritage Center (10am-noon and 1pm-3:30pm Tues.-Fri., 1pm-3:30pm Sat.-Sun.) documents the history of the order and this community through museum displays. The Sisters of Loretto welcome retreatants. Those seeking solitude and reflection should inquire about staying in one of the seven Cedars of Peace cabins on campus.

Accommodations and Food

Although **Hill House Bed and Breakfast** (110 Holy Cross Rd., 877/280-2300, www.thehillhouseky.com, $105-135) dates to the 1800s, the house has been completely gutted and renovated. Save for the original floors and staircase, Hill House is basically a brand-new house and thus sports completely modern rooms and amenities, though antique furniture and classic stylings make the four queen guest rooms as well as the common areas feel warm and inviting. Guests are not only treated to a delicious breakfast, but are also offered wine and cheese in the afternoon.

Loretto is a very small community. For additional accommodation options, as well as a selection of restaurants, head to Lebanon, which is just a few miles southeast.

Getting There

From Bardstown, the easiest way to get to Maker's Mark, which is about 30 minutes away, is to travel south on KY 49 for 9.6 miles. At this point, KY 49 will turn off to the left, but you'll want to stay straight onto KY 527 and drive 3.7 miles to where it intersects with KY 52. Turn left onto KY 52 and drive 4.4 miles to Burkes Spring Road, which leads back to the distillery. You'll pass through "downtown" Loretto on your way. To reach the Sisters of Loretto, stay on KY 49 when it turns left and follow it for five miles to a T-intersection with Nerinx Road, onto which you'll turn left.

From Frankfort (61 miles; 1.5 hours) or Lawrenceburg (48 miles; 1 hour), take southbound U.S. 127 to westbound Blue Grass Parkway and drive 16.9 miles to KY 555 (Exit 42). Proceed 14.7 miles on KY 555 to KY 152. Turn right onto KY 152, and drive 2.8 miles to KY 429. Turn left onto KY 429 and drive 4.2 miles to Burkes Spring Road, onto which you'll turn right to reach the distillery. From Lexington (65 miles; 1.5 hours), take westbound U.S. 60 to the Blue Grass Parkway and then follow the directions from Frankfort. From Louisville (60 miles; 1 hour 20 minutes), head to Bardstown first and then follow the directions from there.

A nine-mile stretch of KY 49 connects Loretto with Lebanon (15 minutes).

LEBANON

Lebanon likes to call itself the heart of Kentucky, as it's located at the state's geographic center. It's also about the midway point on the Bourbon Trail. Besides being the gateway to Maker's Mark, Lebanon, named for the biblical Promised Land location, is home to the cooperage where many of Kentucky's bourbon barrels originate, as well as a young craft distillery.

Kentucky Cooperage

One visit to a distillery and you'll know how important the barrels are to bourbon making. It wouldn't be bourbon without them. Therefore, to get a full understanding of bourbon, you need to head to **Kentucky Cooperage** (712 E. Main St., 270/692-4674, www.independent-stavecompany.com, tours at 9:30am and 1pm Mon.-Fri., free), where most of Kentucky's bourbon barrels are made. The tour has three stops—one in the stave, where barrels are constructed; one in the finishing room, where the all-important charring is done; and one at the cooper's, where barrels that don't pass inspection are repaired by hand. Informative videos are shown at each stop, filling you in on any processes that you might not see firsthand. Because this is a factory tour, closed-toe shoes are required and cameras are not permitted.

Limestone Branch Distillery

Descended from a long line of distillers, brothers Steve and Paul Beam are carrying on the family tradition at their **Limestone Branch Distillery** (1280 Veterans Memorial Hwy., 270/699-9004, www.limestonebranch.com, 10am-5pm Mon.-Sat., 1pm-5pm Sun.), which opened in 2012. While their first batches of bourbon age, the micro-distillery is focusing on single-barrel batches of fruit-flavored moonshine (also called sugarshine). The free half-hour tours, which depart on the hour, take you into the one room where the whole operation is currently centered, allowing you to see the 150-gallon hand-hammered copper still, the fermentation barrels, and the bottling area. Tours end with a tasting. Limestone Branch is a fun diversion from the larger bourbon distilleries, allowing you to experience a much smaller operation and taste something a bit different.

WhiteMoon Winery

Lebanon might be a small town, but they've got all your drinking needs covered—bourbon, moonshine, and now, thanks to **WhiteMoon Winery** (25 Arthur Mattingly Rd., 270/865-4564, 10am-6pm Mon.-Sat.,

1pm-5pm Sun.), wine as well. In the hilly countryside between Maker's Mark and Limestone Branch, WhiteMoon Winery is producing red, white, and rosé wines, ranging from dry to sweet. Stop in to sip some wines while enjoying the scenic views.

Marion County Heritage Center

Through artifacts and rotating exhibits, the **Marion County Heritage Center** (120 W. Main St., 270/699-9455, 10am-4pm Mon.-Fri., 10am-1pm Sat., free) documents the history of the region all the way up to the present day, which means it includes an entire section dedicated to Turtleman (aka Ernie Lee Brown, Jr.), the Lebanon native now known to Animal Planet viewers everywhere.

Lebanon National Cemetery

Designated a national cemetery in 1867, the land that became **Lebanon National Cemetery** (20 KY 208, sunrise-sunset daily) was first used to bury 865 Union dead from the 1862 Battle of Perryville. Since then, service members from all of the United States's wars have been, and continue to be, interred here. Take a stroll on the somber grounds to remember the sacrifices made by soldiers standing in defense of the United States. Services take place on Memorial and Veterans Day, and the cemetery participates in the Wreaths Across America program in December.

Agritourism

Lebanon is surrounded by agricultural land, with farmers growing crops and raising livestock on acres of rich soil. Many of these farms welcome visits by the public, although because they are all working farms, they do ask that visitors make arrangements in advance.

Alpacas have become a popular farm animal in recent years, and at **Serenity Farm** (1380 Frogg Lane, Raywick, 270/692-8743 www.alpacasatserenityfarm.com), owner Tim Auch will gladly show you around and introduce you to his animals. More common to Kentucky are horses, which you can find at **Meadow Creek Farm** (KY 49 & KY 84, 270/692-0021).

Although Kentucky is best known for its thoroughbred horses, the area around Lebanon is standardbred territory, and Meadow Creek produces the best standardbreds around, including world champion Sportswriter.

One of many such displays in the state, the **Marion County Quilt Trail** takes visitors on a tour of the countryside in search of 45 quilt patches decorating barns and other structures. Pick up a brochure at the Lebanon visitors center for more information on each of the designs as well as suggestions for other sites to look for along the way. You'll even learn how to identify different breeds of cow.

Tours

Because Lebanon was home to a train depot and Union Commissary, it felt the wrath of Confederate General John Hunt Morgan on all three of his Civil War raids into Kentucky. A self-guided walking or driving tour points out sites of interest located along the **John Hunt Morgan Trail**. After completing this tour, head to nearby Bradfordsville to explore the **William Clark Quantrill Trail,** a route that commemorates sites related to the notorious outlaw's guerilla attacks.

Architecture buffs may prefer the **Historic Homes & Landmarks Tour,** which offers separate walking and driving tours and points out buildings of note, many of which date to before the Civil War. Brochures with maps for all tours are available at the visitors center.

Nightlife

Once a famous party town thanks to the former Club 68, which hosted the likes of Tina Turner, CCR, and Little Richard, Lebanon is no longer as wild as it once was, but the town still knows how to have a good time. To get in on the fun, set your sights on **Chasers** (110 N. Proctor Knott Ave., 270/699-2221, 4:30pm-1am Mon.-Sat.) or **McB's Bar and Grill** (212 W. Main St., 270/692-3970, http://mcbsbargrill.webs.com, 9pm-1am Tues. and Thurs.-Sat.).

Festivals and Events

Lebanon complements their nightlife with a

BARDSTOWN

packed schedule of festivals, oftentimes putting on two or three events at once. Check the tourism website for a full listing of festivals.

The year's biggest event is **Marion County Country Ham Days** (www.visitlebanonky.com), held on the last weekend of September. In addition to offering all the country ham a person could possibly consume, the festival features the PIGasus parade, a hog calling contest, a car show, carnival, 5K race, and live entertainment.

Fans of radio-controlled planes won't want to miss the weeklong **Jets Over Kentucky** (www.visitlebanonky.com), which takes place at the Lebanon-Springfield Airport in early July. As many as 200 pilots put their jets to the test in dogfights, aerobatic competitions, and other contests. Spectators are welcome to enjoy the show and chat with pilots.

Beat the winter doldrums by attending the **Kentucky Bluegrass Music Kickoff** (www.visitlebanonky.com), which features jam sessions, workshops, and a Saturday night concert headlined by big names in bluegrass. The kickoff is held on a Friday and Saturday in January.

Recreation

Two fishing spots are located just outside downtown Lebanon. Both **Fagan Branch Reservoir** (370 Fagan Branch Rd.) and **Marion County Sportsman's Lake** (716 Sportsman Lake Rd.) are stocked with largemouth bass, smallmouth bass, bluegill, and other popular species. At Fagan Branch Reservoir, you'll also find the Cecil L. Gorley Naturalist Trail, a 3.2-mile loop around the lake that has a notable 43 bridges. The grounds at Sportsman's Lake are open for deer, squirrel, and waterfowl hunting, and also contain archery and skeet ranges.

Take in a 100-mile view that encompasses three counties at **Scott's Ridge Lookout** (KY 84). From a maintained perch, you can look out over a wide swath of farmland, the panorama seemingly endless. The view takes on remarkably different characteristics with each season.

Accommodations

Apparently even John Hunt Morgan and his Raiders found the classic home that is now **Myrtledene Bed and Breakfast** (370 N. Spalding Ave., Lebanon, 270/692-2223, www.myrtledene.com, $95) to be beautiful, as they spared it during their raids through the state. In fact, instead of setting it on fire, they turned it into their headquarters while in Lebanon. Reserve either the queen room or the room with two twin beds, and enjoy the sense of history preserved in the B&B, which is furnished in antiques. On a nice day, take advantage of the grounds, which are complete with fish ponds, hammocks, and swings. Should the weather not cooperate, the rooms are fully equipped with television and wireless Internet, and the house has a library and piano.

Those looking for a standard hotel should book a room at the **Hampton Inn** (1125 Loretto Rd., 270/699-4000, www.hamptoninn.com, $99), which is fresh and clean and provides all the modern amenities. A free all-you-can-eat hot breakfast is offered each morning.

The **Rosewood Cabins** (520 Fairway Dr., 270/692-0506, www.rosewoodgolfcourse.com) are an excellent choice for families or groups of friends, as each cabin has two bedrooms with two double beds in each, as well as a living room and a kitchenette. Golfers will particularly enjoy these cabins because they are located on a course, and cabin rental allows for unlimited golf. A one-night stay is $100, with nightly rates decreasing the longer you stay.

Food

For breakfast or lunch, check out **Joe's Deli on Main** (101 S. Spalding Ave., 270/321-4033, www.joesdelionmain.com, 7am-4pm Mon.-Fri., 8am-2pm Sun., $1.50-7.99). Lighter eaters can choose a breakfast biscuit sandwich, while those who like to start their day with a hearty meal will want to consider the biscuits and gravy, pancakes, or traditional breakfast of eggs, bacon or sausage, potatoes, and biscuit or toast. For lunch, choose from deli sandwiches and wraps, hot sandwiches, burgers, chicken tenders, and salads.

The people behind **Ragetti's Fine Italian Dining** (213 W. Main St., 270/692-1322,

11am-9pm Mon.-Thurs., 11am-10pm Fri.-Sat., noon-9pm Sun., $5.95-10.95) have transformed a former Hardee's into a cozy restaurant decorated with old photos of Lebanon. You'll find hearty pastas, filling pizzas, and a broad selection of subs and strombolis on the menu. Half-portions are available at lunch, and unless you skipped breakfast, it's more than enough food to take you to dinner.

If you're looking for a little flavor in your life, consider **La Fuente** (784 W. Main St., 270/692-3800, 11am-10pm Sun.-Thurs., 11am-10:30pm Fri.-Sat., $5.25-11.99). Though you might wonder how good a Mexican restaurant in the heart of Kentucky can be, you'd be wrong not to give it a chance. Thanks to the area's agricultural nature, a significant population of Hispanics call Lebanon home, and the food at La Fuente is made to please. Lunch specials, which include tacos, tamales, enchiladas, chalupas, and tostadas, start at $3.75.

Information and Services
Tucked away on the second floor of the former junior high school, in what is now called Centre Square, the friendly folks at the **Lebanon Tourist & Convention Commission** (239 N. Spalding Ave., Ste. 200, 270/692-0021, www.visitlebanonky.com, 8am-5pm Mon.-Fri.) will gladly help you plan your visit to Lebanon.

Getting There and Around
From Bardstown (35 minutes), take eastbound U.S. 150 about 15 miles to southbound KY 55, which will, after an additional 9 miles, land you on Lebanon's Main Street. If you're coming from Frankfort or Lexington (both 1.25 hours), take westbound Blue Grass Parkway to southbound KY 555 (Exit 42). After about 15 miles, KY 555 becomes KY 55; continue straight for another 9 miles to reach Lebanon.

Lebanon is located along U.S. 68, which is designated a scenic highway in Kentucky. It begins in Western Kentucky near Illinois, and then travels east and northeast, passing through Land Between the Lakes, Bowling Green, Lexington, and many smaller towns in between before exiting into Ohio at Maysville. If you're

looking for a scenic driving route, U.S. 68 is a good one. Locally, you can take it to reach Perryville and Harrodsburg in the Lexington and Horse Country region of the state.

When driving around the area, be particularly watchful for deer as they are abundant in the area and dangerous to motorists. If you see one cross the road, proceed with extreme caution because others are usually nearby.

LAWRENCEBURG
Lawrenceburg specializes in the fine things in life, which here in Kentucky are bourbon, wine, and cigars made with Kentucky tobacco. Visitors are invited to tour sites related to all three, and no one's going to stop you from taking as many souvenirs of each with you as you'd like. Within easy reach of Frankfort, Lawrenceburg is a small town with a quaint downtown surrounded by farmland.

Four Roses Distillery
Well-known in the United States in the first half of the 20th century, Four Roses then dropped off of most people's radar for the rest of that century as it became an export-only product, sold in Europe and Japan but not in its home country. However, that all changed in 2003, when it came back on the domestic market, and since then, Four Roses' 10 bourbons have caught on big-time. Learn more about the bourbons on a tour of the **Four Roses Distillery** (1224 Bonds Mill Rd., 502/839-3436, http://fourrosesbourbon.com), which is notable for its Spanish Mission-style architecture. Complimentary tours depart on the hour 9am-3pm Monday-Saturday and noon-3pm Sunday. Because the aging warehouses and bottling facilities are located off-site in Clermont, the tour is shorter than those offered at other distilleries, but it does end with a tasting of three different bourbons.

Wild Turkey Distillery
The tour ($5) at **Wild Turkey Distillery** (1525 Tyrone Rd., 502/839-2182, www.wildturkeybourbon.com) provides one of the most in-depth looks at the process by which raw grains

© THERESA DOWELL BLACKINTON

Four Roses is known for its unusual Spanish Mission-style architecture.

are turned into smooth bourbon, though the facilities are a bit more industrial than some of the others. After watching a short film featuring master distiller Jimmy Russell, who has been at Wild Turkey for more than 55 years, visitors witness production step-by-step. Watch a grain truck empty its load, see the yeast starter and grain mash being pumped into the fermenter, poke your head into vats in various stages of fermentation, compare the bourbon-to-be after the first and the second condensation and distillation, and observe the filling of barrels. A new visitors center and upgraded facilities were being added in 2013. Tours are offered on the hour 9am-3pm Monday-Saturday year-round and noon-3pm Sunday, March-November.

Lovers Leap Vineyards & Winery

With 30 acres of vines set on a total of 66 acres, **Lovers Leap Vineyards & Winery** (1180 Lanes Mill Rd., 502/839-1299, www.loversleapwine. com, 11am-6pm Wed.-Sat., 1pm-5pm Sun.) is scenically set on the hills above the Kentucky River. The Leet Family, who bought the vineyard in 2008 and do every step from growing the grapes to bottling the final product on-site, produce white, blush, red, and dessert wines that have medaled at competitions in California, New York, Texas, and Kentucky. Stop in for a tour and tasting.

Rising Sons Winery

With 10 acres of grapes located on their 45-acre family-run winery, **Rising Sons Winery** (643 N. Main St., 502/600-0224, www.risingsons-winery.com, 11am-7pm Sat., 1pm-5pm Sun.) offers visitors the chance to indulge in wine while relaxing on the farm. Rising Sons produces four dry reds, one semisweet red, one semisweet white, one sweet white, and a blackberry dessert wine.

Kentucky Gentlemen Cigars

At **Kentucky Gentlemen Cigars** (1056 Ninevah Rd., 502/839-9226, www.kentuckygentlemencigars.com, 10am-5pm Mon.-Sat.), two of Kentucky's most heralded products—bourbon and tobacco—are combined to make cigars that have gotten the attention of cigar fans around the nation and world. To make the hand-rolled cigars, tobacco is aged for six months in used bourbon barrels. Though the bourbon cigars are most popular, Kentucky Gentlemen Cigars also produces moonshine, mint julep, wine, and other flavored cigars. Stop by to see the production process and learn about this Kentucky Proud business.

Events

Exalting burgoo, a spicy barbecue-style stew popular in Kentucky, the **Anderson County Burgoo Festival** (www.kentuckyburgoo.com) is held annually in Lawrenceburg on the last weekend of September. The main point of the festival is to sample as much burgoo as you can handle, but for a little balance, live music, art and history exhibitions, pageants, and tractor pulls are also on the schedule.

Accommodations

Lawrenceburg Bed & Breakfast (643 N. Main St., 502/930-8242, http://lawrenceburgbb.com, $125) accommodates guests in two spacious suites, each with king bed and private bathroom. For larger groups, an extra room is available, but it shares the bathroom with a suite. Guests are treated to a four-course gourmet breakfast as well as wine and cheese in the afternoon and home-baked desserts in the evening, which can be enjoyed on the large and inviting front porch.

Food

€ Heavens to Betsy (124 Main St., 502/859-9291, 11am-6pm Tues.-Fri., 11am-4pm Sat., $6.75-8.50) is the place to stop for lunch along the Bourbon Trail. The menu is deceptively simple—nine cold sandwiches, five hot sandwiches, two soups, and an assortment of side salads—but the sandwiches are enormous and made with the finest ingredients. It's not uncommon to hear someone say "best sandwich ever" after they finish their reuben or the H2B pretzel panini, which features deli ham, beer cheese, and mild banana peppers on a pretzel bun. You might feel too full for dessert, but you'll still want to get a piece of cake—take it to go if you must.

Information and Services

The **Anderson County Tourism Commission** (502/517-6362, www.visitlawrenceburgky.com) can provide you with information on Lawrenceburg. While in town, stop into City Hall (100 N. Main St., 9am-5pm Mon.-Fri.), where tourist information is available in the foyer of the historic building.

Getting There and Around

Lawrenceburg lies at the intersection of U.S. 62 and U.S. 127. It's about 15 miles (25 minutes) south of Frankfort on U.S. 127, and about 25 miles (40 minutes) west of Lexington if you take U.S. 60 to Versailles and then switch to U.S. 62. From Bardstown (45 minutes), travel 34 miles on eastbound Blue Grass Parkway to northbound U.S. 127, which after 5 miles will lead to Lawrenceburg. If you're coming from nearby Danville (30 miles; 40 minutes) or Harrodsburg (20 miles; 25 minutes), just follow northbound U.S. 127.

BARDSTOWN

KENTUCKY DISTILLERIES, BIG AND SMALL

Created by the Kentucky Distillers Association, the Bourbon Trail is an official route that was put together as a means of drawing tourists to member distilleries. It does not, however, include all of the distilleries in the state, many of which are located in the area covered by this chapter, the heart of the bourbon distilling area, but some of which are located elsewhere. For those wishing to be comprehensive in their distillery touring, the list below covers all of Kentucky's major bourbon distilleries and their locations, moving from west to east.

· Evan Williams Bourbon Experience (www.evanwilliams.com), Louisville

· Jim Beam Distillery (www.americanstillhouse.com), Clermont

· Heaven Hill Distillery (www.heavenhill.com), Bardstown

· Barton 1792 Distillery (www.1792bourbon.com), Bardstown

· Maker's Mark Distillery (www.makersmark.com), Loretto

· Four Roses Distillery (www.fourrosesbourbon.com), Lawrenceburg

· Wild Turkey Distillery (http://wildturkeybourbon.com), Lawrenceburg

· Buffalo Trace (www.buffalotrace.com), Frankfort

· Woodford Reserve Distillery (www.woodfordreserve.com), Versailles

· Town Branch Distillery (www.kentuckyale.com), Lexington

In addition to the major distilleries, Kentucky is also home to multiple craft distilleries, not all of which make bourbon. Some focus specifically on other spirits (moonshine being particularly popular); some produce bourbon in addition to other spirits. These craft distilleries and their locations, again from west to east, are as follows.

· Silver Trail Distillery (http://lblmoonshine.com), Hardin

· MB Roland Distillery (www.mbrdistillery.com), Pembroke

· Corsair Artisan Distillery (www.corsairartisan.com), Bowling Green

· Willett Distillery (www.kentuckybourbonwhiskey.com), Bardstown

· Limestone Branch Distillery (http://limestonebranch.com), Lebanon

· Barrel House Distillery (http://barrelhousedistillery.com), Lexington

New distilleries continue to pop up throughout the state. At the time of research, the following distilleries had plans to open to the public for tours and tastings.

· Angel's Envy Distillery (www.angelsenvy.com), Louisville

· Michter's Distillery (www.michters.com), Louisville

· Nth Degree Distillery (www.nthdegreedistilling.com), Bellevue

All distilleries that were open at the time of research, big and small, receive full write-ups in the relevant chapters of this guidebook.

© THERESA DOWELL BLACKINTON

Willett Distillery

Frankfort

A favorite Kentucky joke asks "How do you pronounce the capital of Kentucky: Loo-IS-ville or Loo-EE-ville?" And while neither of those is the correct way to pronounce Louisville, the joke is that no matter how you pronounce it, Louisville is not the capital of Kentucky. Small, unassuming Frankfort is actually the capital of the Bluegrass State. Unlike many state capitals, Frankfort is neither big nor bustling. Sure, when government is in session, there's a bit more traffic on the roads and in the restaurants, but life still goes on at a measured pace and remains overwhelmingly hassle-free. Though politics can be ugly, Frankfort is charming. Attractive historic buildings line downtown streets, through which trains still pass daily; a "singing" bridge helps traffic move across the Kentucky River, which flows right through the city; and a plethora of parks preserve tracts of lush land perfect for picnicking, hiking, biking, and wildlife watching.

GOVERNMENT SIGHTS
Kentucky State Capitol
The **Kentucky State Capitol** (700 Capital Ave., 502/564-3449, http://capitol.ky.gov, 8am-4:30pm Mon.-Fri., 10am-2pm Sat., free), a beaux arts building with classical French influences throughout, celebrated its centennial in 2010. Visitors to the capitol will first notice the statues in the first-floor rotunda, which represent important figures in Kentucky history: President Abraham Lincoln, Statesman Henry Clay, Dr. Ephraim McDowell, Vice President Alben Barkley, and President of the Confederacy Jefferson Davis. Each level of the government occupies a floor of the capitol: The executive branch is located on the first floor, the judicial branch on the second, and

© THERESA DOWELL BLACKINTON

inside the Kentucky State Capitol

BARDSTOWN

BARDSTOWN

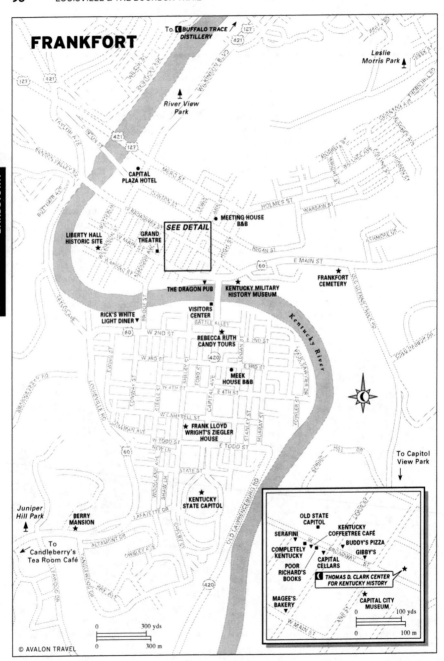

FRANKFORT

To BUFFALO TRACE DISTILLERY

Leslie Morris Park

River View Park

CAPITAL PLAZA HOTEL

MEETING HOUSE B&B

SEE DETAIL

LIBERTY HALL HISTORIC SITE

GRAND THEATRE

FRANKFORT CEMETERY

THE DRAGON PUB

KENTUCKY MILITARY HISTORY MUSEUM

RICK'S WHITE LIGHT DINER

VISITORS CENTER

BATTLE ALLEY

Kentucky River

REBECCA RUTH CANDY TOURS

MEEK HOUSE B&B

FRANK LLOYD WRIGHT'S ZIEGLER HOUSE

To Capitol View Park

KENTUCKY STATE CAPITOL

Juniper Hill Park

BERRY MANSION

To Candleberry's Tea Room Café

OLD STATE CAPITOL

KENTUCKY COFFEETREE CAFÉ

SERAFINI

BUDDY'S PIZZA

COMPLETELY KENTUCKY

GIBBY'S

CAPITAL CELLARS

POOR RICHARD'S BOOKS

THOMAS D. CLARK CENTER FOR KENTUCKY HISTORY

MAGEE'S BAKERY

CAPITAL CITY MUSEUM

0   100 yds

0   100 m

0   300 yds

0   300 m

© AVALON TRAVEL

the legislative branch on the third. In addition to visiting the House and Senate chambers and the Supreme Court, don't miss the State Reception Room on the second floor, which puts one in mind of the Palace of Versailles thanks to its mirrors and chandeliers as well as its intricate decor. Visitors can ask for a map at the tour desk or download it from the website and explore the capitol on their own, or inquire about guided tours being offered that day. An ID is required for admission.

The grounds of the capitol are notable in their own right, designed by the Olmsted brothers, sons of legendary landscape architect Frederick Law Olmsted. The **Capitol Grounds Walking Tour** brochure, available at the desk inside the capitol or on the capitol website, outlines a route with stops at 37 sites. One of these stops is at the **Floral Clock**, which measures 34 feet across and is filled seasonally with more than 10,000 plants.

The Executive Mansion (www.governorsmansion.ky.gov), home to the governor and his family, is also located in the capitol complex. The mansion, built in the same beaux arts style as the capitol and specifically fashioned after one of Marie Antoinette's villas, is one of only a handful of executive residences in the nation that are open to the public. Free tours are offered 9am-11am on Tuesday and Thursday, but require an appointment (502/564-3449) and may be canceled if an event is being held at the mansion.

MUSEUMS AND HISTORICAL SIGHTS
◖ Thomas D. Clark Center for Kentucky History

As the one and only museum dedicated to Kentucky history—12,000 years of it—the **Thomas D. Clark Center for Kentucky History** (100 W. Broadway, 502/564-1792, http://history.ky.gov, 10am-4pm Wed., 10am-8pm Thurs., 10am-5pm Fri.-Sat., $4 adults, $2 youth 6-18) is home to a rich collection of artifacts, a portion of which are displayed in the center's permanent exhibit, with others appearing in temporary exhibits. The permanent exhibit, A Kentucky Journey, tells the story of the state era by era with the help of authentic items as well as hands-on activities and animatronic characters. Don't miss Museum Theater, an impressive performance series in which on-staff actors write and present short plays about various aspects of Kentucky history. Performances take place on Saturday afternoons at 1pm and 3pm as well as at varying times during the week. Check the online calendar for the current schedule. Admission to the center also includes admission to the Old State Capitol and the Kentucky Military History Museum.

Genealogists will want to visit the center's **Martin F. Schmidt Library,** which is the premier center for Kentucky genealogy research. Family history workshops held 6:30pm-7:30pm every Thursday help those interested in tracing their roots establish a plan and identify resources.

Old State Capitol

Because the plans for the current state capitol required more space than was available at the site of the third capitol (the first two burned down), the **Old State Capitol** (Broadway and St. Clair St., 502/564-1792, http://history.ky.gov, 10am-4pm Wed., 10am-8pm Thurs., 10am-5pm Fri.-Sat., $4 adults, $2 youth 6-18) was not demolished when the new capitol was opened in 1910, and to this day still stands as a monument to history. Designed by Gideon Shyrock and meant to resemble a Greek temple, the Old State Capitol was built out of Kentucky marble (aka limestone) and was considered architecturally advanced when completed in 1830. The circular staircase, held in place by a single keystone, is indeed remarkable and a must-see for architecture buffs. Tours take you into the House and Senate chambers, furnished mainly in reproduction furniture but with original paintings; the library; the court chambers; and the first-floor office rooms, which house an exhibit on the capitol lawn—host to everything from cattle to concerts. Admission to the Old State Capitol also includes admission to the Thomas D. Clark Center for Kentucky History and the Kentucky Military History Museum.

BARDSTOWN

© THERESA DOWELL BLACKINTON

Old State Capitol

Kentucky Military History Museum

After a five-year renovation, the Old State Arsenal has opened as the **Kentucky Military History Museum** (125 E. Main St., 502/564-1792, http://history.ky.gov, 10am-4pm Wed., 10am-8pm Thurs., 10am-5pm Fri.-Sat., $4 adults, $2 youth 6-18), with exhibitions that detail Kentucky's involvement in conflicts from the War of 1812 to the recent engagements in Iraq and Afghanistan. Artifacts and oral histories from veterans help visitors get a sense of military history. Admission to the Kentucky Military History Museum also includes admission to the Thomas D. Clark Center for Kentucky History and the Old State Capitol.

Capital City Museum

Housed in the former Capital Hotel, which dates to the 1850s, the **Capital City Museum** (325 Ann St., 502/696-0607, www.capitalcitymuseum.com, 10am-4pm Mon.-Sat., free) presents the story of Frankfort, from the founding of the town on the Kentucky River to its successful bid to become the state capital to its current state. Photos, artifacts, and life-size dioramas make the history accessible and interesting in this small museum.

Liberty Hall Historic Site

Built at the end of the 18th century for U.S. Senator John Brown, **Liberty Hall** (202 Wilkinson St., 502/227-2560, www.libertyhall.org, tours at noon, 1:30pm, 3pm Tues.-Sat., spring-fall, $6 adults, $5 seniors, $2 youth 5-18) was one of the first brick buildings in Frankfort and remains an important landmark. The neighboring Orlando Brown House, though built in the Greek revival style, also belonged to Senator Brown, who had it built in 1835 so that each of his sons would inherit a house. Today, hour-long tours take visitors through both properties, with guides helping to interpret history, architecture, and decor through the story of the Brown family. The tour doesn't include the grounds, but you should pad your schedule so that you have time

© THERESA DOWELL BLACKINTON

bourbon tasting at Buffalo Trace

to wander the lawn and gardens, which lead down to the Kentucky River.

Berry Mansion

Once owned by a wealthy family involved in the whiskey industry, the 22-room **Berry Mansion** (700 Louisville Rd., 502/564-3449, www.historicproperties.ky.gov, 8:30am-4pm Mon.-Fri., free), built from stone quarried on the property, now houses government offices and hosts special events, including weddings. Tours, which include highlights of the foyer, dining room, library, drawing room, music room, service wing, and grounds, can be scheduled through the capitol tour desk at the listed phone number. Go ahead and gawk at the large pipe organ in the ornate music room; that room alone, which was added in 1912, cost nearly as much as the entire Executive Mansion.

Frankfort Cemetery

Though governors, artists, military heroes, and the developer of Bibb lettuce all rest eternally at **Frankfort Cemetery** (215 E. Main St.,

502/227-2403, dawn-dusk), the burial ground's most famous residents are the Boones: Daniel and his wife, Rebecca. Though both Boones died and were buried in Missouri, they were brought back to Kentucky and interred in Frankfort in 1845. A tall rectangular monument, which stands on a bluff overlooking the Kentucky River and the capitol, marks their shared grave. Pick up a map and brochure at the information center or just follow the signs to Daniel Boone's grave.

BOURBON SIGHTS

⟨ Buffalo Trace Distillery

Thanks to the fact that it was allowed to remain open during Prohibition as one of four distilleries authorized to produce "medicinal" liquor, **Buffalo Trace Distillery** (1001 Wilkinson Blvd., 502/696-5926, www.buffalotrace.com) owns the title of the oldest continually operating distillery in America. A complimentary tour of Buffalo Trace starts with a short video that relays the history of the region and the distillery; continues with a peek at Warehouse D, where the 13 different bourbons made at the distillery are aged; segues into a visit to the line where premium bourbons are hand-bottled; and ends with a tasting, where you can choose two tastes from a selection that will include a couple of bourbons as well as other spirits made at the distillery. Tours, which depart on the hour, are offered 9am-4pm Monday-Saturday year-round and noon-3pm Sunday April-October.

In addition to the standard tour, Buffalo Trace also offers a Hard Hat Tour (10:30am and 1:30pm Mon.-Fri. and 10:30am Sat.), which shows the step-by-step process by which bourbon is made—from grain delivery through fermentation and distillation. Architecture and history aficionados will want to sign up for the National Historic Landmark Tour (11:30am Mon.-Fri.), which focuses on the growth that took place at Buffalo Trace from 1930 to 1950 as Americans were once again allowed to legally consume alcohol. Believers in the supernatural will want to check out the Ghost Tour (7pm Thurs.-Sat.), on which you'll hear stories of the ghosts said to haunt the distillery and see some of its spookier sites. All three of the specialty tours are complimentary, but they do require reservations.

Rebecca Ruth Candy Tours
Thanks to the creation of the now-famous bourbon ball, products from **Rebecca Ruth Candy** (112 E. 2nd St., 502/223-7475, www.rebeccaruth.com, 10am-noon and 1pm-5:30pm Mon.-Sat., Apr.-Nov.) are enjoyed around the country and even internationally. The business didn't start out with such global aspirations, however. Instead, it was founded by two substitute schoolteachers, Ruth Hanly and Rebecca Gooch, who decided they had more of a knack for making candy than for teaching. Your sweet tooth will agree. Take a 20-minute tour ($3) of the small facility (which somehow manages to produce more than three million pieces of candy each year) to learn about the history of the business and the women, see the century-old stove where candy is made, and hear the story of how an offhanded comment led to the development of their signature candy. Samples are included on the tour.

OTHER SIGHTS
Salato Wildlife Education Center
Run by the Department of Fish and Wildlife, the **Salato Wildlife Education Center** (1 Sportsman Ln., 502/564-7863, http://fw.ky.gov, 9am-5pm Tues.-Fri., 10am-5pm Sat., $4 adults, $2 youth 5-18) seeks to teach visitors about Kentucky ecosystems and the creation and protection of wildlife habitats. Start your visit in the exhibition hall, where you can check out live snakes, frogs, and fish and dioramas of larger stuffed animals. Then hit the paved path for a circuit that will take you through a diversity of habitats and past large, natural enclosures housing eagles, black bears, elk, bison, bobcats, and deer. Those looking for a little more adventure will want to lace up their hiking books and explore the 0.5-mile red-blazed HabiTrek Trail, which connects with the 0.2-mile yellow-blazed Prairie Trail, or try out the three-mile white-blazed Pea Ridge Loop Trail.

The complex also offers two fishing lakes and picnic areas, so pack your lunch and make it a day. There is no fee to access the hiking trails, lakes, and picnic areas.

Kentucky State University
Created in 1886 to provide higher education to Kentucky's African Americans, **Kentucky State University** (400 E. Main St., 502/597-6000, www.kysu.edu) remains proud of its heritage while now serving a diverse student body. Visitors to the campus will want to stop in the Jackson Hall gallery and lobby, as well as the Visitor and Information Center in the Carroll Academic Services building to see rotating exhibitions culled from the collections of the Center of Excellence for the Study of Kentucky African Americans. A Kentucky Civil Rights Hall of Fame, which honors 52 inductees, can be viewed in the Carl Hill Student Center Ballroom. Campus maps are available at the Visitor and Information Center.

Kentucky Vietnam Veterans Memorial
The **Kentucky Vietnam Veterans Memorial** (300 Coffee Tree Rd., www.kyvietnammemorial.net) honors the 125,000 Kentuckians who served in the conflict, including the 1,103 who were killed. The design, by architect and veteran Helm Roberts, is unusual: The memorial is a very large sundial. The base, which is granite, is inscribed with the names of those who lost their lives and is patterned in such a way that on the anniversary of their death, the shadow of the sundial pointer falls on their name. Verses from Ecclesiastes are also inscribed in the base.

Frank Lloyd Wright's Ziegler House
Architecture fans will want to drive by the **Ziegler House** (509 Shelby St.), which was designed by architect Frank Lloyd Wright in his famous prairie house style. Though the clean-lined white house is distinctive, it fits in seamlessly on the street, on which a number of impressive houses of varying styles are located.

KENTUCKY'S DRY COUNTIES

As the number one producer of America's only native spirit, Kentucky appears on the surface to be a state that likes its liquor. Dive deeper, and you'll see that alcohol sales are a contentious issue in the Bluegrass State. After all, Carrie Nation, the radical hatchet-wielding leader of the temperance movement, was a Kentuckian.

Although most Americans consider it their right in post-Prohibition America to buy alcohol anywhere so long as they are of legal age, that's not the case in Kentucky. Only 32 of Kentucky's 120 counties are wet, meaning that alcoholic beverages can be sold by businesses for on-site or off-site consumption. A surprising 39 counties are completely dry, meaning alcohol sales are prohibited throughout the entire county. The remaining 49 counties are "moist," which means they are primarily dry, but they may have a city that is completely wet (such as Bowling Green in Warren County), have cities that allow sales by the drink in certain restaurants, or have golf courses or wineries that are allowed to serve alcohol.

Dry areas can be found in every region in the state, although they are most concentrated in southern, eastern, and far western Kentucky, which are Bible Belt areas, and the ban on alcohol has everything to do with religious beliefs. In these areas especially, you'll have to go a long way before you find alcohol—at least legal alcohol, that is. Moonshine is alive and well in Kentucky, despite what officials may try to tell you. It should be noted that it is not illegal to possess alcohol for private consumption in dry counties; it is simply illegal to sell it. The majority of the wet counties are in the vicinity of Louisville, Lexington, Northern Kentucky, and Owensboro. Not only are these the state's most populated and urban areas, but they also have strong Catholic communities. Interpret that how you will.

A map showing the distribution of wet and dry counties is available through the website of the Kentucky Department of Alcoholic Beverage Control (http://abc.ky.gov).

A historical marker indicates the house, which is private and may only be viewed from the street. The Ziegler House is the only Wright-designed house in Kentucky.

Switzer Covered Bridge

One of only a handful of covered bridges remaining in Kentucky, the **Switzer Covered Bridge** (KY 1262 and KY 1689) is a 120-foot-long Howe truss bridge built in 1855 to span the Elkhorn River. In 1954, the bridge was closed to traffic, a concrete structure taking its place. Restored multiple times since its construction, the bridge can now be crossed by foot, and though the external structure is in good condition, graffiti scars the interior.

ENTERTAINMENT AND EVENTS
Nightlife
Frankfort is not really known for its nightlife.

Many government workers head back to their hometowns on weekends, while locals often opt to see what's going on in nearby Lexington. Standalone bars are few and far between, but many restaurants buzz in the evenings with locals seeking out a drink and entertainment. The bar at Serafini, for instance, is always crowded.

The hottest place in town for a drink is **Capital Cellars** (227 W. Broadway, 502/352-2600, http://capitalcellars.net, 10am-9pm Mon.-Thurs., 10am-10pm Fri.-Sat.). It's where people come together, especially those interested in arts, culture, and meeting new friends. With an enormous selection of wines at reasonable prices ($4-6 per glass; a bottle can be enjoyed in-store for $2 over retail), as well as a short menu of sandwiches, salads, and snacks such as cheese plates, olive trays, and smoked salmon, it's a great place to grab a light dinner, then hang out, as art exhibitions open, musicians start impromptu jam sessions, and people meet and mingle. For those not inclined toward wine, Capital Cellars also offers 35 Kentucky bourbons as well as a wide choice of other drinks.

Though the **Kentucky Coffeetree Café** (235 W. Broadway, 502/875-3009, www.kentuckycoffeetree.com, 7am-9pm Mon.-Wed., 7am-10pm Thurs.-Fri., 8am-10pm Sat., 8am-7pm Sun.) serves up coffees, smoothies, sandwiches, and pastries during the day, on weekend evenings it's the place to go for live music. The intimate setting makes it feel as if the musicians are playing just for you. Some performances are ticketed; others require a cover. Check the website for details.

For a more traditional bar experience, grab at table at **The Dragon Pub** (103 W. Main St., 502/875-9300, www.dragonpub.com, 11am-2am Mon.-Fri., 10am-1am Sat.), where Tuesday night is trivia night and Fridays and Saturdays feature live music. Expect a young professional crowd, ready to relax after work.

Performing Arts

Built in 1911 as a small vaudeville theater, the **Grand Theatre** (308 St. Clair St., 502/352-7469, www.grandtheatrefrankfort.org) was converted into a large movie theater in the 1940s before closing in 1966. Now, thanks to a group of activist citizens, the Grand is back as a community arts center. In addition to again showing films, the theater also hosts art exhibitions, concerts, and other performances. Check the online schedule for upcoming events and ticket information.

Festivals and Events

Head to the lawn of the Old State Capitol for the **Summer Concert Series** (www.downtownfrankfort.com) every other Friday in the summer at 7pm. Bring a blanket, bring a friend, bring a picnic; entertainment is provided.

On the first weekend of June, Frankfort shows off its goods at the **Capitol Expo Festival** (www.capitalexpofestival.com). The three-day event includes a cornhole tournament, a lip sync contest, a fireworks show over the Kentucky River, an arts and crafts show, and lots of live music.

SHOPPING
Bookstores

Bookstore lovers will delight in **Poor Richard's Books** (233 W. Broadway, 502/223-8018, http://poorrichards.indiebound.com, 10am-6pm Mon.-Fri., 10am-5pm Sat., 12:30pm-5pm Sun.), where the front shelves are dedicated to Kentucky authors while the rest of the store contains popular offerings in every genre. It's nearly impossible to leave without a new read in hand.

Kentucky Products

From horse brooches to carved wooden benches, **Completely Kentucky** (237 W. Broadway, 502/223-5240, www.completelykentucky.com, 9:30am-6pm Mon.-Fri., 9:30am-5pm Sat., 12:30pm-5pm Sun.) covers the entire spread of Kentucky-made arts, crafts, and souvenirs. Items range from the decorative (glass pieces and prints) to the useful (ceramic dishes) to the mouthwatering (gift baskets of Kentucky food) to the absurd (junkyard animals). There's something for everyone.

For other unique local products, be sure to check out the gift shops at the Center for Kentucky History and Buffalo Trace Distillery.

SPORTS AND RECREATION
Parks

Stop at **River View Park** (Wilkinson Blvd., across from Capital Plaza) for a walk along a one-mile path that runs parallel to the Kentucky River. Sixteen sites of historical interest are marked along the trail. The park also offers a fishing pier, boat dock, and picnic area, and hosts the farmers market May-October.

Juniper Hill Park (800 Louisville Rd., 502/696-0607, www.frankfortparksandrec.com, 7am-11pm, Apr.-Oct., 7am-dusk, Nov.-Mar.) offers some of the best recreational facilities in the city with an Olympic-size pool, sand volleyball courts, tennis courts, and an 18-hole golf course. You'll also find extensive picnic facilities and a playground at Juniper Hill.

shops of downtown Frankfort

Pull over at the **scenic overlook** on U.S. 60 as you head out of downtown Frankfort and go toward Louisville for an excellent view of the capitol, which sits directly in front of and below the overlook.

Hiking

Start your visit to **Cove Spring Park** (100 Cove Spring Rd., 502/696-0607, www.frankfortparksandrec.com, 8am-11pm Apr.-Oct., 8am-dusk Nov.-Mar.) with a stop at the waterfall located right next to the parking lot, then create a hiking route from the park's four trails and multiple connectors. No matter what path you choose to use to explore the park's 100 acres, you'll pass through riverine forest that is home to deer, wild turkeys, great blue herons, and other wildlife.

From Fort Hill, Frankfort militia protected the city from an attempted Confederate invasion in 1864. Today, **Leslie Morris Park** (400 Clifton Ave., 502/696-0607, www.frankfortparksandrec.com, dawn-dusk daily) preserves the remains of the forts built on this hill and allows visitors to experience them on a series of trails that loop through acres of forest, where deer and other wildlife are known to live. A brochure available from a box in the parking lot outlines a 0.6-mile route that takes you past many of the sites and provides a wonderful panorama of the entirety of Frankfort. Those looking for a good workout can actually ascend the hill from the city via the Old Military Road Walking Trail, which begins behind the Capital Plaza tower.

Biking

Capital City Cycles (475 Versailles Rd., 502/352-2480, http://capitalcitycyclesky.com, 10am-6pm Mon.-Sat., noon-5pm Sun.) is Frankfort's go-to place for all biking needs. The shop services and sells bikes and also rents road, mountain, and hybrid bikes by the day and week. Staff members are avid cyclists and can answer any question you have about where to bike in Frankfort, and the store also organizes group rides. Call or stop in for more information.

In addition to soccer and softball fields, **Capitol View Park** (Glenns Creek Rd., 502/696-0607, www.frankfortparksandrec.com, 8am-11pm, Apr.-Oct., 8am-dark, Nov.-Mar.) features 10 miles of mountain bike trails. The trails run along the river and through the woods and connect to make one large loop.

Water Sports
The Kentucky River and Elkhorn Creek offer excellent canoeing and kayaking waters, and there's no outfitter better suited to help get you out on those waters than **Canoe Kentucky** (7323 Peaks Mill Rd., 888/226-6359, www.canoeky.com). They offer instruction for those new to the activity, sales for those who can't get enough, and both guided and self-guided boat trips for paddlers of all levels. Options range in length and distance, from short evening paddles in the moonlight to all-day trips. Children are welcome, but if they weigh less than 35 pounds, you'll have to provide your own life jacket for them. All activities should be booked in advance.

Horseback Riding
A Little Bit of Heaven Riding Stables (3226 Sullivan Ln., 502/223-8925, www.kystable.com) offers horseback riding lessons on their Appaloosa horses. No experience is necessary, but you do need to call ahead to arrange a lesson. Because of the size of the horses, a weight limit of 185 pounds is strictly enforced. Those too timid to climb onboard are welcome to take a tour of the paddock and meet the nearly 50 horses boarded there.

ACCOMMODATIONS
$50-100
The **Capital Plaza Hotel** (405 Wilkinson Blvd., 502/227-5100, www.capitalplazaky.com, $89-99) offers 189 guest rooms outfitted with standard hotel amenities, including cable television and wireless Internet, and decorated in standard, but now somewhat dated, hotel style. Located next to the convention center, the hotel is popular with business travelers, but

is also within walking distance of Frankfort's main sights.

$100-150
Built prior to the Civil War, ◖ **The Meeting House Bed and Breakfast** (519 Ann St., 502/226-3226, www.themeetinghousebandb.com, $115-125) retains many of the features of the original building, including the poplar floors, the walnut banister on the three-floor staircase, the high ceilings, and the many fireplaces. Period pieces throughout the house, which is located within easy walking distance of most attractions, add to the historic feel. The house has been updated, however, so that each of the four guest rooms has its own private bath with walk-in shower. Rooms are large with desks and comfortable chairs and feature cable TV and wireless Internet. Three rooms have full beds and one has a queen. Homemade cookies are served each afternoon, and breakfast is served in courses. Scottish eggs are the house specialty. Don't let the Boston accent of hosts Gary and Rose throw you; they know more about Frankfort than many of its lifelong residents.

The bathroom attached to the Red Room at **Meek House Bed and Breakfast** (119 E. 3rd St., 502/227-2566, www.bbonline.com, $115) was, in its last incarnation, most likely a bedroom. It's that big. It features a claw-foot tub and walk-in shower and even has its own door to the patio overlooking the tranquil garden. The bedroom is itself quite large, with plenty of open space left despite the room having a king-size bed and loveseat. The B&B's other room, the Green Room, is perfect for traveling partners who prefer separate beds as it contains two twins as well as a pull-out couch. Both rooms have stocked refrigerators and TVs. At the multicourse breakfast, you might be treated to a Mexican quiche, herbed eggs with cheese on an English muffin, or cinnamon chip French toast, as well as a starter course of yogurt and homemade granola.

A number of chain hotels are located in Frankfort, including a **Hampton Inn** (1310 U.S. 127 S., 502/223-7600, www.hamptoninn.com,

$109) and a **Best Western** (80 Chenault Dr., 502/695-6111, www.bestwesternkentucky.com, $104), both of which offer nice rooms with all the amenities one would expect. Although each is convenient to I-64, neither is located in the heart of the city.

Campgrounds

RVers will be happy with the services at **Elkhorn Campground** (165 N. Scruggs Ln., 502/695-9154, www.elkhorncampground. com), which offers 125 sites, 61 of which have full hookups. For entertainment, choose from the campground's pool, mini-golf facility, horseshoe pit, basketball and volleyball courts, and playground. Located on the banks of the Elkhorn, the location is peaceful as well as convenient to Frankfort sites.

Those more interested in outdoor offerings than historic sites will want to check out **Still Waters Campground** (249 Strohmeier Rd., 502/223-8896, www.stillwaterscampground. com), which is located on the Kentucky River and features boat ramps and offers canoe and kayak rentals. In addition to full-service sites, the campground has two primitive camping areas.

FOOD
Farmers Market
Fresh fruits, vegetables, and assorted other agricultural products are available for purchase at the **Frankfort Farmers Market** (River View Park, 7am-noon Tues., Thurs., and Sat.) three times each week.

Cafés and Bakeries
Candleberry's Tea Room & Café (1502 Louisville Rd., 502/875-0485, www.candleberrytearoom.com, 11am-2pm Tues.-Fri., $5.95-7.95) offers light lunches served in a cozy atmosphere. Take your pick from a list of sandwiches or daily quiche and soup specials. If you can't decide, they'll let you mix and match. Finish your meal with a perfectly sweet piece of chess pie, said to be made from a vintage recipe. Of course, you'll want to have tea with your meal—the only trouble is you have to pick from

a long, tempting list. For the true tea connoisseur, book a reservation 48 hours in advance for afternoon tea on Saturday ($18.95), where you'll be treated to scones, soup, and a selection of sweet and savory goodies to go along with your tea. It's perfect for an outing with the girls or a mother-daughter date, though men are plenty welcome.

For a breakfast treat or an afternoon sweet, visit **Magee's Bakery** (225 W. Main, 502/223-7621, http://frankfortmagees.com, 7am-2pm Tues.-Fri., 8am-2pm Sat.) and choose from a tasty selection of fresh-baked doughnuts, cookies, cupcakes, breads, tarts, pies, and other pastries. Magee's also offers a small menu of sandwiches, wraps, and soups at lunch.

Casual American
Although **Gibby's** (204 W. Broadway, 502/223-4429, www.eatatgibbys.com, 10:30am-9pm Mon.-Sat., $3.49-14.99) offers pasta, meat, and seafood entrées, it's primarily known for filling sandwiches and stuffed spuds. Located in the revitalized downtown, Gibby's does a bustling lunch business, popular with locals looking for a quick, tasty lunch before heading back to work.

Fans of the old-fashioned diner, where the chef/owner has a colorful history and the gift of gab, won't want to miss **◖ Rick's White Light Diner** (114 Bridge St., 502/696-9104, www.whitelightdiner.com, 11am-5pm Tues.-Fri., 8am-3pm Sat., $7.75-19.50). The menu leans toward Cajun, with crawfish pie, a variety of po' boys, and a New Orleans muffuletta all finding a spot on the menu. Though the space and style is traditional decor, the food is high-quality, with local meats, eggs, and produce used whenever possible. Food Network fans might recognize the place from *Diners, Drive-Ins, and Dives.*

Italian
Hole-in-the-wall **Buddy's Pizza** (212 W. Broadway, 502/352-2920, 11am-9pm Mon.-Thurs., 11am-10pm Fri., noon-9pm Sat., $8-17.50) offers the best pies in town. Choose from a specialty pizza or create your own combo to

BARDSTOWN

be baked to perfection in Buddy's brick oven. Salads and Italian sandwiches ($4-7) round out the menu. At lunch on weekdays, pizza is available by the slice ($2.50).

Serafini (243 W. Broadway, 502/875-5599, www.serafinifrankfort.com, 11am-3pm Mon.-Fri. and 4:30pm-10pm Mon.-Sat., $15-36) is Frankfort's nicest restaurant, serving up an excellent selection of pastas and meat and fish dishes. The menu changes seasonally, but might feature Shanghai scallops, grilled filet mignon, or a pork chop marinated in sweet tea. The risotto of the day is always a good choice. Desserts are decadent, so consider sharing. Tall booths provide privacy, though you can also opt for an open table or even open-air seating when the weather is nice. At lunch ($8-13), the menu runs primarily to pastas, sandwiches, and pizzas.

INFORMATION AND SERVICES

Located in a beautiful Queen Anne-style house, the **Visitors Center** (100 Capital Ave., 502/875-8687, www.visitfrankfort.com, 8am-5pm Mon.-Fri., 9:30am-2:30pm Sat. May-Sept.) stocks brochures and maps, and the friendly staff can provide you with information on dining and hotel options in Frankfort and Franklin County. The center also offers free wireless Internet.

A **post office** is located at 1210 Wilkinson Boulevard, near Buffalo Trace Distillery.

GETTING THERE

Frankfort is located just north of I-64. From Louisville (one hour), take eastbound I-64 for nearly 50 miles to northbound U.S. 127 (Exit 53B), which will lead into downtown Frankfort after about 5 miles. From Lexington (45 minutes), you can take westbound I-64 for 21 miles to westbound U.S. 60 (Exit 58). After 2.5 miles, U.S. 60 will hit Main Street. If you prefer to avoid the interstate or are on the western side of Lexington, drive 20 miles on northbound U.S. 421, at which point you'll hit Main Street. From Bardstown (one hour), travel on eastbound Blue Grass Parkway for 34 miles

to northbound U.S. 127 (Exit 59B). Then drive an additional 16 miles, passing through Lawrenceburg, to reach Frankfort.

Frankfort is 315 miles (4.75 hours) from St. Louis (4.75 hours) via eastbound I-64; 165 miles (2.5 hours) from Indianapolis via southbound I-65 to Louisville and then eastbound I-64; 80 miles (1.5 hours) from Cincinnati via southbound I-71 and southbound U.S. 127; and 210 miles (3.25 hours) from Nashville via northbound I-65 and eastbound Blue Grass Parkway.

Frankfort's Capital City Airport is not served by commercial airlines. The nearest airports are Blue Grass Airport in Lexington and Louisville International Airport.

GETTING AROUND
Public Transportation

Listen for the friendly ring of Frankfort's free **downtown trolley** (www.visitfrankfort.com, 10am-3pm Tues.-Fri.), then hop onboard to enjoy old-fashioned transport among the city's most popular sites. Among the many stops are the Capitol, Rebecca Ruth Candy, Frankfort Cemetery, The Center for Kentucky History, Liberty Hall, River View Park, and Buffalo Trace Distillery. Departures are scheduled at 40-minute intervals, making the trolley a fun and convenient way to see Frankfort.

Tours

Multiple walking tours of Frankfort are offered throughout the year. **Russ Hatter's Downtown Tour,** which costs $5 for adults and is free for those under 12, provides an in-depth look at Frankfort history. Call 502/696-9127 for reservations. Those who delight in the fact that trains still run right through Frankfort will be interested in **Chuck Bogart's Railroad Walking Tour,** an hour-long trip through railroad history. Reservations for the free tour can be made by calling 502/227-2436. Naturalists will want to sign up for **Russ Kennedy's Kentucky River Walk,** a free tour focusing on the history of the river and its impact on Frankfort. Call 502/803-0242 for reservations. If you're visiting Frankfort during the witching month, get in the mood for Halloween with a **Murder and Mayhem Tour,** held every Thursday night in October at 7:30pm. Guides, costumed like early 20th-century policemen, tell tales of 30 grisly Frankfort murders while leading a tour through the nighttime streets of Frankfort. The tour, which costs $10 and departs from the Capital City Museum, is restricted to those 18 and older. Reserve a spot on the tour by calling 502/696-0607.

For those who prefer to tour at their own pace, walking and driving tour brochures are available at the visitors center. To uncover the stories behind the many historic buildings that form the heart of downtown Frankfort, request a copy of the **walking tour brochure.** Brief histories of 40 different sites, all within a 10-block radius, are provided in the brochure. Civil War buffs will want to pick up a copy of the **Civil War Driving Tour** brochure and follow the route to 15 sites with connections to the war. All sites are within the city, so driving distances are short, but the tour is long on interesting facts.

Versailles and Midway

Woodford County, home to the towns of Versailles and Midway, produces some of the finest products to come out of Kentucky—Woodford Reserve bourbon and thoroughbred racehorses. Both the towns are small but wealthy and offer food and accommodation of a quality that far exceeds their size. Versailles—which is pronounced Vur-SALES because this is Kentucky and not France—is the bigger of the two cities, named in honor of General Lafayette, a friend of the city's founder. Midway, which isn't much more than a main street and a whole lot of surrounding farmland, was Kentucky's first railroad town. It is strategically situated midway (hence its name) between Frankfort and Lexington. Both towns are exceedingly charming, and the drive between the two is on a scenic byway lined with gorgeous horse farms. Very close to Lexington, either city makes a good base for exploring the entire region.

HORSE FARMS

Woodford County is home to more than 100 horse farms. At times, while driving around the area, it can seem as if there is nothing else. Everywhere your gaze falls, you'll find stone and wood fences enclosing rolling bluegrass hills dotted with horses. The majority of the farms are closed to the public, though those listed here welcome visitors with advance reservations.

Ashford Stud

Derby winners Fusaichi Pegasus and Thunder Gulch are two of the stallions that stand in the distinctive blue-trimmed barns at **Ashford Stud** (5095 Frankfort Rd., Versailles, 859/873-7088, www.coolmore.com). Free tours of the breeding complex at this beautiful facility are offered by reservation. The horses may travel south during the latter half of the year, so aim to visit Ashford Stud between February and June if possible.

Lane's End

Outside of the breeding season, **Lane's End** (1500 Midway Rd., Versailles, 859/873-7300, www.lanesend.com) offers free tours of their stallion complex at 10am on Thursdays July-January. Meet the horses, learn about the industry, and admire Lane's End's park-like setting. Among the more well-known horses on-site is Curlin, a two-time Horse of the Year. The facility hosts a couple of open houses each year, which are open to both breeders and the public. Check the website to find out if an open house is on the schedule.

Three Chimneys Farm

Three Chimneys Farm (1981 Old Frankfort

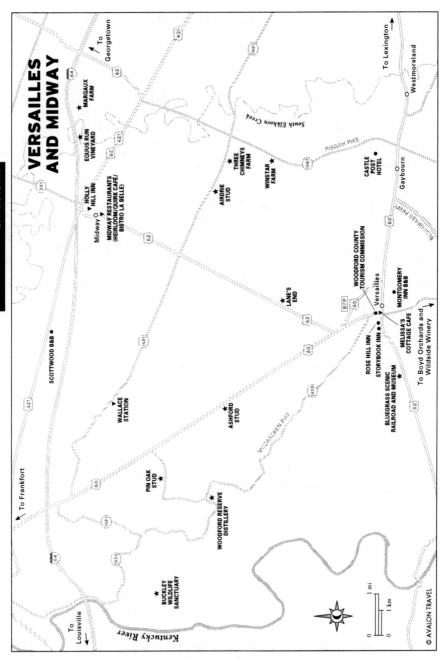

VERSAILLES AND MIDWAY

Pike, Versailles, 859/873-7053, www.three-chimneys.com, 1pm Tues.-Sat., $10) has been home to a long list of thoroughbreds that any horse racing fan will know, including Seattle Slew, Silver Charm, Genuine Risk, and Big Brown. Kentucky Derby 2008 winner Big Brown is currently standing stud at Three Chimneys Farm and is often brought out and walked for visitors. If a breeding session is scheduled during your visit, you may be allowed to watch. With notable stone architecture and lush green fields, Three Chimneys Farm is not just a premier stud farm, but also a pretty place to tour.

WinStar Farm

For an insider's look at how champion thoroughbred horses are bred, visit **WinStar Farm** (3301 Pisgah Pike, Versailles, 859/297-1328, www.winstarfarm.com), owner of 2010 Kentucky Derby winner Super Saver. Tours begin with a video that features 2000 Horse of the Year Tiznow. Visitors then move into the stallion complex, where they are introduced to the farm's stallions, including attention-loving Tiznow, and are informed about the process of breeding. Guides can answer any and all questions you might have about thoroughbreds, racing, breeding, sales, and training, so don't be shy. Free tours are offered at 1pm Monday, Wednesday, and Friday.

Additional Farms

Other horse farms that provide free tours of their facilities include **Airdrie Stud** (2641 Old Frankfort Pike, Midway, 859/873-7270, www.airdriestud.com), **Margaux Farm** (596 Moore's Mill Rd., Versailles, 859/846-4433, www.margauxfarm.com), and **Pin Oak Stud** (830 Grassy Springs Rd., Versailles, 859/873-1420, www.pinoakstud.com).

BOURBON DISTILLERIES AND WINERIES

Woodford Reserve Distillery

Though Woodford Reserve bourbon has been produced only since 1996, the **Woodford**

Reserve Distillery (7855 McCracken Pike, Versailles, 859/879-1812, www.woodfordreserve.com), the National Historic Landmark where it is made, is one of the oldest distilleries in the state. Join a one-hour tour for an in-depth look at the process by which this premium bourbon, the official bourbon of the Kentucky Derby, is made. You'll see the only stone aging warehouses in America, learn that Woodford Reserve is the only bourbon to be distilled three times before being barreled, and visit the only bourbon fermenting facility to use wood tanks exclusively. Tours end with a tasting, and visitors are allowed to take their shot glass home with them. Tours ($7) are offered on the hour 10am-3pm Monday-Saturday year-round, with additional tours at 1pm, 2pm, and 3pm on Sundays April-December. Two specialty tours ($25)—a National Landmark Tour, which focuses on the distillery's architecture, and a Corn to Cork Tour, which is a more in-depth look at the bourbon-making process—are also offered, but they require advance reservations.

Equus Run Vineyards

Nestled between horse farms and South Elkhorn Creek, **Equus Run Vineyards** (1280 Moores Mill Rd., Midway, 859/846-9463, www.equusrunvineyards.com, 11am-7pm Mon.-Sat., 1pm-5pm Sun. Apr.-Oct., 11am-5pm Mon.-Sat., 1pm-5pm Sun. Nov.-Mar.) has been producing award-winning wines since 1998. A complimentary guided tour is offered at 1:30pm Monday-Thursday and at 1:30pm and 4pm Friday and Saturday. Guests who arrive outside those hours are welcome to take a self-guided tour of the grounds. Regardless of whether you take a tour, tastings ($5), which include six wines and a souvenir glass, are offered until 15 minutes before closing. The vineyard produces 15 red, white, and rosé wines, and as the official wine of the Derby, also creates special-edition wines each year. A number of events are held at the vineyard, including a very popular summer concert series. Check the website for a schedule of upcoming events.

BARDSTOWN

BARDSTOWN

© THERESA DOWELL BLACKINTON

thoroughbreds on the horizon at a horse farm

Wildside Winery

Wildside Winery (5500 Troy Pike, Versailles, 859/879-3982, www.wildsidevines.com, 1pm-7pm Tues.-Sat., 1pm-5pm Sun.) makes a long list of wines, focusing especially on dry red and sweet fruit wines. In addition to the usual strawberry and blackberry, Wildside also does peach mead, cranberry, and pomegranate wines, plus a few other less common selections. Among the reds, you'll find a syrah, a cabernet sauvignon, and a cynthiana, along with a bourbon barrel red, which is a cabernet that is aged in a bourbon barrel. A couple of whites are also available. Tastings are free, and the winery occasionally hosts outdoor concerts.

OTHER SIGHTS

Bluegrass Scenic Railroad and Museum

Get a taste of rail travel on a one-hour train ride with **Bluegrass Scenic Railroad and Museum** (175 Beasley Rd., Versailles, 859/873-2476, www.bluegrassrailroad.com, 1pm-4pm weekends). The rides, which are offered at 2pm on weekends mid-May-October, take passengers through the bluegrass countryside. You'll pass through Trackside Farm, where thoroughbreds are raised, and see cattle, tobacco fields, and other rural Kentucky sites. Special train rides are held throughout the year and include Civil War train robbery rides, mystery theater rides, haunted Halloween rides, and a Christmas ride with Santa. Come early or hang around after the ride to explore the one-room museum, which has exhibits on the work the railroad did for the United States, the jobs of those who worked for the railroad, and the trains that used to pass through the area. Tickets ($11.50 adults, $10.50 seniors, $9.50 youth 2-12) can be purchased online or in person. Plan to arrive 30 minutes before departure, because trains here run on a Swiss timetable, departing right on schedule.

Boyd Orchards

As fifth-generation fruit growers, the Boyd family knows a little something about fruit, and a visit to **Boyd Orchards** (1396 Pinckard Pike, Versailles, 859/873-3097, www.boydorchards.com, 9am-6pm Tues.-Sat., noon-6pm Sun.) is a treat for your taste buds. The only problem is that after tasting their strawberries, peaches, apples, blackberries, raspberries, grapes, and pears, you might be too spoiled to ever again settle for grocery store produce. Beyond producing mouthwatering fruit that you can purchase already picked or head to the fields to pick yourself, Boyd Orchards also has an enormous playground and animal area ($5) that kids love and a great gift shop full of unique products. During the seven weeks leading up to Halloween, Boyd Orchards hosts an extremely popular fall festival with a petting zoo, live music, corn maze, face painting, pony rides, mini-train rides, hayrides, and of course, plenty of pumpkins, mums, and gourds. Their **Apple Blossom Café** has a full kitchen that turns out tasty lunches that often feature fruit fresh from the farm. Try the fruit slushes and the sandwiches and salads built around the produce of the moment (maybe a strawberry goat cheese salad or a Cuban sandwich with asparagus). For dessert, good luck choosing between apple cider doughnuts and fried apple or peach pies.

RECREATION
Hiking
The **Buckley Wildlife Sanctuary** (1305 Germany Rd., 859/873-5711, www.audubon.org, 9am-5pm Wed.-Fri., 9am-6pm Sat.-Sun., $4 adults, $3 youth) has four trails, ranging in length from 0.3 to 1.5 miles and easily connectable, which lead into field, pond, and forest habitats. A bulletin board in the parking lot has a box filled with binders that provide information on the trails and point out sights you'll encounter along the way. Bird lovers will enjoy the bird blind, which is perched on the edge of a pond that many avian species like to visit. Field guides are provided for identification of species, but bring your own binoculars. The Nature Center is open 1pm-6pm weekends April-December.

BARDSTOWN

© THERESA DOWELL BLACKINTON

Boyd Orchards

ACCOMMODATIONS

Versailles and Midway offer a surprising number of accommodation options, none of which are chains. With their close proximity to Lexington and especially Keeneland, the B&Bs in Versailles and Midway are a good option for those looking to spend time all around the region.

$150-200

Dating back to 1795, the house that is now **⟨ Scottwood Bed and Breakfast** (2004 E. Leestown Pike, Midway, 859/846-5037, www.scottwoodbedandbreakfast.com, $175-195) journeyed from its original location in Scott County to its present location in 1971. An addition was built at that point, but the house maintains the beautiful period woodwork and floors. Two guest rooms are located in the house, one on the main floor, the other occupying the entirety of the second floor. The upstairs suite, which can accommodate a family or group thanks to the twin beds in the room that adjoins the main bedroom, is decorated in Shaker style, while the down bedroom is done in the style of Williamsburg. Both rooms have private baths. A carriage house is located behind the main house and offers a private retreat with working fireplace and a lovely deck overlooking South Elkhorn Creek. Breakfast is provided each morning, and the rooms are equipped with satellite television and wireless Internet.

No one stays at **⟨ Rose Hill Inn** (233 Rose Hill Ave., Versailles, 859/873-5957, www.rosehillinn.com, $139-184) and doesn't love it. The seven tastefully decorated rooms in this historic 1823 home have private baths, comfy beds, and TVs, and come with special touches like robes, homemade cookies, and candles. All rooms are spacious, and the various configurations—kings, queens, twins—can accommodate couples, families, or groups of friends. Some rooms feature whirlpool tubs and kitchen areas, and three of the rooms are even able to accommodate pets. The owners are excellent hosts who serve up a delicious breakfast daily and will do everything in their power to make sure you have a wonderful stay.

The **Montgomery Inn Bed and Breakfast** (270 Montgomery Ave., Versailles, 859/251-4103, www.montgomeryinnbnb.com, $139-179) has 10 guest suites, each with a private bathroom with whirlpool tub, queen or king bed, TV with DVD player, and Internet access. Some have private entryways, and all have access to complimentary snacks and drinks. Rates include a full breakfast. The decor can be a little bit busy, with patterned wallpapers, bed covers, and upholstery overwhelming those with simpler tastes. Those with allergies should be aware that multiple cats call the inn home.

Over $200

⟨ Storybook Inn (277 Rose Hill Ave., Versailles, 859/879-9993, www.storybook-inn.com, $259-325) is an upscale bed-and-breakfast where not a single detail is overlooked. An antebellum-style mansion dating to 1843, Storybook Inn was renovated in 2009-2010. In the inn's four suites, you'll find such niceties as rain showerheads, soaking tubs, towel warmers, and fireplaces, not to mention luxurious linens, mattresses, and furniture. A guesthouse with 3 bedrooms, 3.5 bathrooms, an office that can be used as an additional bedroom, a kitchen, and a private deck is perfect for those seeking privacy or traveling in a group. Common areas include a beautiful garden and a library stocked with books and movies. Homemade treats and refreshments are available all day, and the delicious breakfasts can be tailored to accommodate any restrictions. Innkeeper Elise is a delight and will dedicate her full attention to helping you plan your visit.

It's impossible to drive down Pisgah Pike and not see the **Castle Post Hotel** (230 Pisgah Pike, Versailles, 859/879-1000, www.thecastlepost.com, $195-420). It is, after all, a castle with turrets, 12-foot wooden doors, and stone walls, smack in the middle of horse country. Though there are a lot of people who want to tour it, the only way you can gain admission to the castle is by booking an overnight room. It's not cheap, but how many people can say they've slept in a castle in Kentucky? Rooms are luxuriously decorated (for better or worse, they don't feel at all medieval) and come with all the amenities.

FOOD

You will not go hungry while visiting Versailles and Midway. Locally owned restaurants rule, and they're doing exciting things with food here.

Cafés

For a fantastic sandwich in downtown Midway, pop in at **Bistro La Belle Market + Café** (121 E. Main St., Midway, 859/846-4233, 11am-2pm Tues.-Sat., $6.50), where roasted chicken salad, white cheddar pecan spread, Kentucky country ham, and other sandwich fixings are served on a selection of freshly baked bread.

Casual American

The Big Brown burger at **(** **Wallace Station** (3854 Old Frankfort Pike, Versailles, 859/846-5161, www.wallacestation.com, 8am-8pm Mon.-Thurs., 8am-9pm Fri.-Sat., 8am-6pm Sun., $5.95-8.95) was named a top five burger by Guy Fieri of Food Network's *Diners, Drive-Ins, and Dives,* who visited this deli and bakery in 2010. If you're not into burgers, you can choose from a very long list of sandwiches, all of which are excellent, or opt for soup or salad. A special fried chicken dinner is offered on Mondays, and Fridays feature fried catfish. For breakfast, try one of the country Benedict sandwiches or grab a treat from the bakery. Wallace Station is completely low-key with a few mismatched tables and chairs inside and a number of picnic tables on a deck. Live bluegrass music adds to the ambience on Saturday evenings. A special gluten-free menu is available.

Classic American

Depending on your mood, choose to sit at either the casual and cozy downstairs pub or the more refined upstairs dining room at **815 Prime** (131 E. Main St., Midway, 859/846-4688, www.815prime.com, 5pm-10pm Tues.-Sat., $10-22), both of which serve the same menu of American favorites, which range from a burger, fish and chips, and a prime rib sandwich to a bone-in pork chop, wild-caught walleye, and a New York strip. Though the menu isn't as creative as some in the area, the food is solid, the atmosphere is nice, and the service is good.

Contemporary American

Details matter at **(** **Heirloom** (125 E. Main St., Midway, 859/846-5565, www.heirloom-midway.com, 11:30am-2pm and 5:30pm-9pm Tues.-Sat., $12-33). The dining room is elegant but comfortable, decorated in shades of brown, tan, and white and furnished with extra-tall booths and granite tables. Presentation is an art, with each dish expertly plated on unique dishes, and the tastes are spectacular. The menu is short, featuring about seven entrées, but each is carefully thought out and executed. The menu changes regularly, but might include duck breast with pumpkin ricotta ravioli or capellini with Alaskan king crab. The lunch menu ($9-13) tempts diners with favorites such as buttermilk-brined fried chicken and fish and chips.

Although open only limited hours, **(** **Holly Hill Inn** (426 N. Winter St., Midway, 859/846-4732, www.hollyhillinn.com, 11am-2pm Fri.-Sun., 5:30pm-10pm Thurs.-Sat.) is worth working into the schedule. James Beard-nominated chef Ouita Michel impresses guests with elevated Southern cuisine prepared with local ingredients and served in the charming surroundings of an 1845 country inn. Lunch and Sunday brunch are three-course affairs ($18), in which you choose from such options as local chicken crepes and eggplant *involtini.* The three-course dinner ($35) is built around such entrées as spicy lamb sausage harissa and roulade of beef tenderloin. A six-course tasting menu ($65) is also offered. Reservations are highly recommended at this deservedly popular restaurant.

For a rather unusual dining experience, head out of town to a tiny place called Nonesuch, Kentucky, where you'll find an enormous antiques gallery called Irish Acres. Proceed to the lower level to a restaurant named **The Glitz** (4205 Ford's Mill Rd., Nonesuch, 859/873-6956, www.irishacresgallery.com, 10am-5pm Tues.-Sat.), which makes complete sense when you see the place. The Glitz serves a three-course luncheon menu, with multiple selections for each of the courses. For dessert, you'll want to try the signature dish, the Nonesuch Kiss, which involves a meringue shell, ice cream, chocolate sauce, whipped cream, almonds, and a cherry. The food is carefully prepared, and the atmosphere incomparable. Beverages are included with the meal, which costs $21.50. Reservations are required.

Southern

Fans of comfort food will find refuge at **Melissa's Cottage Café** (167 S. Main St., Versailles, 859/879-6204, 11am-9pm Mon.-Sat., $6.95-11.95), where meatloaf, chicken pot pie, and hamburger steak are some of the most popular entrées. Portions are generous and come with good Southern-style sides. The menu does change often and is presented to you on a chalkboard. Unlike many comfort food spots, Melissa's is a charming (albeit tiny) place with tasteful decor.

INFORMATION AND SERVICES

Stop into the visitor information center run by the **Woodford County Tourism Commission** (190 N. Main St., Versailles, 859/873-5122, www.woodfordcountyinfo.com, 10am-4pm Mon.-Fri.) for information on the area.

GETTING THERE AND AROUND

Versailles is located directly west of Lexington on U.S. 60, which connects the two cities. From the center of Lexington, Versailles is about 13 miles (25 minutes) away, although Versailles is only about 6 miles (10 minutes) from Keeneland, making it equally as convenient as Lexington if you're in the area for horse racing. Midway is north of Versailles, located just south of I-64. To travel between Versailles and Midway, drive 7.5 miles (15 minutes) on westbound U.S. 62. From Lexington, the most direct route to Midway is via northbound U.S. 421. Lexington and Midway are separated by 15 miles (25 minutes). From Louisville and points westward, take I-64 to Exit 58 to reach Versailles (64 miles; one hour) and Exit 65 to reach Midway (60 miles; one hour). From Covington (90 miles; 1.5 hours) and points north or west, travel to Lexington and proceed from there.

MAP SYMBOLS

▦ Expressway	⟨ Highlight	✕ Airfield	⚲ Golf Course
Primary Road	○ City/Town	✈ Airport	℗ Parking Area
Secondary Road	◉ State Capital	▲ Mountain	⬟ Archaeological Site
Unpaved Road	⊛ National Capital	✛ Unique Natural Feature	▮ Church
Trail	★ Point of Interest		▮ Gas Station
Ferry	• Accommodation	Waterfall	Glacier
Railroad	▾ Restaurant/Bar	▲ Park	Mangrove
Pedestrian Walkway	▪ Other Location	▣ Trailhead	Reef
Stairs	⋀ Campground	⛷ Skiing Area	Swamp

CONVERSION TABLES

°C = (°F - 32) / 1.8
°F = (°C x 1.8) + 32
1 inch = 2.54 centimeters (cm)
1 foot = 0.304 meters (m)
1 yard = 0.914 meters
1 mile = 1.6093 kilometers (km)
1 km = 0.6214 miles
1 fathom = 1.8288 m
1 chain = 20.1168 m
1 furlong = 201.168 m
1 acre = 0.4047 hectares
1 sq km = 100 hectares
1 sq mile = 2.59 square km
1 ounce = 28.35 grams
1 pound = 0.4536 kilograms
1 short ton = 0.90718 metric ton
1 short ton = 2,000 pounds
1 long ton = 1.016 metric tons
1 long ton = 2,240 pounds
1 metric ton = 1,000 kilograms
1 quart = 0.94635 liters
1 US gallon = 3.7854 liters
1 Imperial gallon = 4.5459 liters
1 nautical mile = 1.852 km

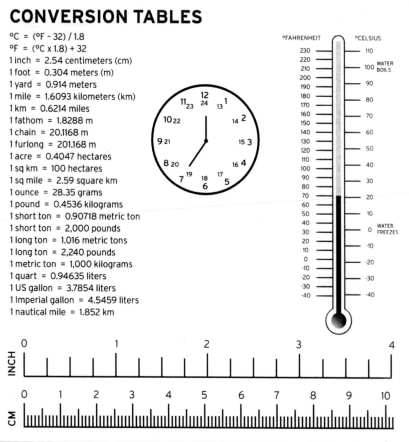

MOON SPOTLIGHT LOUISVILLE & THE BOURBON TRAIL

Avalon Travel
a member of the Perseus Books Group
1700 Fourth Street
Berkeley, CA 94710, USA
www.moon.com

Editor: Nikki Ioakimedes
Series Manager: Kathryn Ettinger
Copy Editor: Melissa Brandzel
Graphics and Production Coordinator: Lucie Ericksen
Map Editor: Kat Bennett
Cartographers: Stephanie Poulain, Brian Shotwell

ISBN-13: 978-1-61238-894-6

Title page photo: Louisville skyline © dndavis/123RF

Printed in the United States of America

ABOUT THE AUTHOR

© JEFF BLACKINTON

Theresa Dowell Blackinton

Theresa Dowell Blackinton was born and raised in Louisville, Kentucky, and spent her childhood visiting the state's attractions with her parents and three brothers. She left Kentucky to attend college at Rice University in Houston, Texas, and has been on the move ever since – living in Freiburg, Germany; Athens, Greece; Washington DC; and Durham, North Carolina; and spending time in more than 50 countries. But she still considers the Bluegrass State home.

While researching this book, Theresa was reminded of Kentucky's interesting history and awesome natural beauty – but what she most enjoyed was getting to interact with her home state's warm and welcoming people, all of whom had interesting stories to tell.

Theresa is the author of Moon *Take a Hike Washington DC* and has written for multiple newspapers and magazines.